D1055577

A Chorus of Wisdom

Notes on Spiritual Living

from...

Gerald G. Jampolsky, M.D.

Larry Dossey, M.D.

Arlo Guthrie

Barbara De Angelis, Ph.D.

Armand DiMele

Dan Wakefield

Judith Light

Gloria Estefan

Bernie Siegel, M.D.

Alan Cohen

Wally "Famous" Amos

Ma Jaya Sati Bhagavati

Neale Donald Walsch

and many more...

edited by Sorah Dubitsky, Ph.D.

MJF BOOKS
NEW YORK

Published by MJF Books
Fine Communications
322 Eighth Avenue
New York, NY 10001

A Chorus of Wisdom
LC Control Number 2006939985
ISBN-13: 978-1-56731-871-5
ISBN-10: 1-56731-871-1

Copyright © 2005 by Sorah Dubitsky.

For full copyright information see page 203.

This edition is published by MJF Books in arrangement with Ulysses Press.

All rights reserved. No part of this publication may be reproduced or transmitted in
any form or by any means, electronic or mechanical, including photocopy, recording, or any
information storage and retrieval system, without the prior written permission of the publisher.

Printed in the United States of America.

MJF Books and the MJF colophon are trademarks of Fine Creative Media, Inc.

QM   10 9   8   7   6   5   4   3   2   1

To Jeanne DeQuine,
thanks for your presence on this planet.

Table of contents

Foreword

Black Elk said that few live in reality but most only in the shadows that reality casts. Our most miraculous journey is to discover our inherent luminosity and call it forth from the shadows.

In this work each author asks of us, as they do of themselves, to look directly into the heart of the body and the mind. This clear seeing is the path toward the center of the greater labyrinth of our lives. It is the accumulation of insights that amount to wisdom, it is the song sung on the path to liberation, the gradual wholeness as our disparate parts unite. Each essay displays the heart of consciousness as it rises into this wounded world, opening unimagined vistas and encouraging deeper commitment and wider engagement in the well-being of others.

There is an energy transmitted when a woman or man of wisdom speaks into the heart of an aspirant. In the writings or direct communications with such a person we may gain something we have been longing for, and if the transmission is pure enough—without much ego taint—one may learn something greater of oneself, find an unrecognized need for a life of the spirit. One may receive an opening of a yet deeper level of our inherent wisdom.

The best teachers turn us on to ourselves. They offer tools for self-discovery and the encouragement to employ them with as much ardor as the heart can muster, reordering our priories. It's like a person drowning who is struggling to reach the surface—that yearning of the spirit—that homesickness for our boundless essence is like that. It yearns to be free of the obstacles to wisdom and the heart. The spirit gradually sheds the weight that can floor it, loosing the restraints of conditioning and the fears of the unknown, rising toward the light.

Those that Sorah has invited to the platform of *A Chorus of Wisdom* all are teachers and their teachings have touched her heart. In this compilation, this beckoning toward the light, Sorah shares the words that she recognizes as healing, as well as her own constantly expanding heart.

Stephen and Ondrea Levine
Chamisal, New Mexico
April 2005

Introduction

■ SORAH DUBITSKY, PH.D.

When I was twenty-six years old, I wound up hospitalized with a stomach ulcer. Naively, I viewed my ulcer as a minor interruption, an irritation, something to be ignored and forgotten in my otherwise perfect life. I really believed my life was perfect, for I had everything that my mother, father, and society had taught me to want and attain: perfect husband, perfect house, perfect job, and perfect income. It wasn't until years later when I realized that twenty-six-year-olds, who have a perfect life, don't have stomach ulcers. I realized that the ulcer was symptomatic of an underlying emptiness that had been eating away at me for years. The emptiness surfaced from time to time in occasional introspective tirades of "who am I, where am I going, what am I doing?" But I swallowed these thoughts and kept on going. Again, it wasn't until years later that I learned that the emptiness I was experiencing was really a lack of spiritual nourishment.

Many of the essays in *A Chorus of Wisdom: Notes on Spiritual Living* appeared as interviews in the magazine Miracle Journeys, which I published for seven years. The collective wisdom found in this book is written by people who, in one form or another, have been teachers, way-showers or guides to me. Their words have helped me navigate life's stormy waters more smoothly. In the process, I'm becoming the person I'm meant to be. And, miraculously, I'm no longer empty.

To me, spiritual living is living with the awareness that I'm part of something far greater. It is called by many names in many different disciplines. Some call it God, intelligence, universal energy, nonlocal mind, Spirit, consciousness or pure awareness. The Kabbalah says it's no-thing, and so can't be called anything at all. Quantum physics calls it the field out of which the entire universe is created. Eastern mysticism calls it *chi* or *prana*. It can also be called Life Force. It's the core essence we hear in the silence of our own hearts.

Spiritual living is like being on a roller coaster, knowing that you are strapped safely into your seat. Or it's like canoeing on an unknown river. The river goes fast, slow, turns into rapids and waterfalls, and sometimes it seems like you're barely hanging on, but it will carry you to where you're supposed to be if you just lie back and let it. When you start to live with the awareness that your reality is spirit, you become happier, lighter, and less stressed out. The great psychologist Abraham Maslow called the experience of connecting to spirit as a peak experience. People who have had peak experiences are self-actualized. A definition of self-actualization is "having no needs." Having no needs doesn't mean you stop making money or eating or sleeping. It means that you have a basic trust that life will bring you what you need. People who are self-actualized are innovators and pioneers. They are living their lives on their own terms because they realize there is nothing to be afraid of. They realize that to live in accordance with their highest calling is what spiritual living is about.

There's a saying that when the student is ready, the teacher appears. The contributors to this book have all been teachers to me. They have reminded me, in one way or another, to remain focused on the still small voice of the spirit within me. The contributors are seekers in their own right. The themes they talk about are based on their experiences. And so they are more than experts or authorities. They are also people just like you and me who have opened up to spirit and are living their lives with more certainty, peace, and fulfillment.

The essays are arranged in seven sections, which reflect different aspects of spiritual living. In the first section, Personal Journey, Gloria Estefan, Arlo Guthrie, Nathan Katz, Judith Light, Toby Thompkins, and Dan Wakefield share their journeys and ideas about what it means to be spiritual. The next section, Manifesting Your Dreams, offers essential advice from Marc Allen, Jack Canfield, Rev. Edwene Gaines, and John Perkins, on creating the life you want. The section on Spiritual Relationships and Sexuality, with essays by Diane Cirincione and Gerald G. Jampolsky, Ondrea and Stephen Levine, and Armand DiMele, goes to the core of how to create unconditionally loving relationships. There's also an essay by Hans Christian King who assures us that a loving God does not punish anyone for his or her sexuality. Spiritual Awareness, the section featuring Wally "Famous" Amos, Steve Bhaerman, Barbara De Angelis, Larry Dubitsky, and Debbie Ford, describes insights and tools for living with more awareness. In the section on Healing, Larry Dossey and Caroline Myss talk about the changing spectrum of health care, while Rabbi Chaim Richter talks about healthy aging. The section titled Changing the World, contains essays from Ma Jaya Sati Bhagavati, Alan Cohen, Jean Houston, Stephen Simon, and two essays from Neale Donald Walsch, that remind us we don't live in a vacuum: we can make a difference. The last section, Living with Mortality, with essays by Gerald G. Jampolsky, Bernie Siegel, and James Van Praagh addresses the fears associated with knowing one's time here is finite. And yet, although we are physically finite, spiritually we're infinite.

At the end of each essay there is a passage "For Reflection," a meditation or self-awareness exercise for integrating the main point of each essay into your everyday life. Spiritual living is developed through step-by-step daily practice. It is a lifelong process. It is a journey of self-healing.

Take time with this book. Think about it. Use the "For Reflection" tools. Allow this book to inspire you to spend more time cultivating a spiritual life.

May the collective wisdom in *A Chorus of Wisdom* enlighten your path, as it has mine.

personal
journey

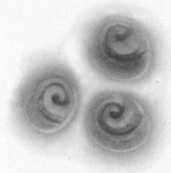

What it means to be spiritual

■ GLORIA ESTEFAN

Gloria Estefan's passion is to bring joy to her audiences. Estefan, who along with her husband, Emilio, and their Miami Sound Machine, put Miami on the map as a center for creativity. Gloria's music crosses cultures and generations. She captures the universal chord of the human spirit. With over thirty top-ten singles in categories ranging from Latin to R & B, Gloria has amassed enough hit records to have recorded two greatest-hits albums. Not only has she dominated the music world, but she's also gone into acting, playing a teacher in the movie *Music of the Heart*, which starred Meryl Streep. Currently this prolific artist is working on a movie, TV show, and two new albums.

Gloria is a genuine humanitarian who has expressed that bringing joy to people is the greatest reward she can receive. Through the Gloria Estefan Foundation, she has made a commitment to supporting education, art and music programs, and children's programs. Her work on behalf of her own community of Miami demonstrates that. Everyone who was there in 1992 will remember the concert she organized at the Joe Robbie Stadium that raised over $4 million for the rebuilding effort after Hurricane Andrew. She also spearheaded a campaign that raised over $40 million to develop and build the Lois Pope Life Center, which houses the Miami Project to Cure Paralysis.

Gloria's spiritual journey has been about developing inner strength and then using that strength in the service of inspiring humanity.

After many experiences that have tested me throughout my life, I have come to the conclusion that the purpose of adversity is to teach us and make us stronger. If we are never challenged, we cannot grow spiritually, mentally, and emotionally. I'm even thankful for those who have tried to cause me harm because they have taught me patience and compassion. I also firmly believe that "thoughts create reality." I work very hard to make sure my thoughts are positive and focus on the way I want my life to be rather than simply accepting what, on the surface, seems to be my destiny. The song "Coming Out of the Dark" was written to thank the countless people that loved and supported me through a very difficult time after a bad accident I had in 1990 that left me paralyzed from the waist down. I "felt" people's prayers as a physical energy surrounding me and used their beautiful intentions in my daily healing process. I truly believe all those incredible vibrations of unconditional love were instrumental in a recovery that my doctors called no less than "miraculous." I think that as we learn more about the incredible healing capabilities that we all possess, miracles will become more and more commonplace.

To me "Spirit" is the essence of "All" there is. I believe we are each a "fragment" of what most of us call "God." Because of this we have boundless possibilities and creativity. I like to think of my spirit as a tree made up of roots, trunk, boughs and leaves. My spirit is the entire tree, whereas this life that I'm living now may be perhaps only a leaf on that tree, living a completely different reality from all the other parts. By going inward, as in meditation, I try to access the entire memory of the tree in all its collective yet different experiences. I try to connect with the higher self that is more in tune to the "Big Picture."

I think the beauty of music is that it is a combination of different "vibrations." Since we are all pure energy we are touched by music almost as if it goes "through" us. It doesn't really matter what language the lyrics are in, in order for music to make us "feel" something. My lyrics also touch on subjects that unite us rather than divide. They usually deal with emotions that are prevalent in all our different cultures and races.

Creativity is one of the most rewarding ways to connect with our sense of spirit. My most fulfilling moments have come when another person tells me that my song helped them through a crisis or made them feel happy. I've been told on more than one occasion that a certain song I wrote stopped someone from committing suicide or helped them reestablish a bond with a loved one. What more could anyone ask than to affect someone's life without ever having met them. It's wonderful to know that there are certain things in existence that are here because we are here.

I see the entertainment industry creating something close to "Mass Meditation." That's why it's important that we supervise the violent content that our children are exposed to on a daily basis. These things desensitize us and allow for far more "possibilities" to be acted out. As creative beings we will create both in the positive and negative spectrums.

I am committed to giving back because it is what fulfills me the most. I am most happy when I can make someone else happy. I try to instill a sense of responsibility in my children as well, so they see how fortunate we are to be able to help others.

I think that the more we become aware that we are all collectively creating the "realities" on this earth, the quicker we will be able to affect positive change. If we realize that we are all connected and never alone regardless of how things might "look" to us, we will feel more responsible for each other's happiness. I believe we are here not only to enjoy the wonderful and delicious experiences available to us in this physical world, but also to learn to love each other unconditionally. After all, what else is there of any real value?

for reflection

Gloria Estefan wrote the song "Coming Out of the Dark" as an offering of gratitude to the people who loved and supported her through her difficult times.

Gratitude is the most healing emotion we can have. Expressing gratitude to others is a wonderful way to make ourselves both healthier and happier.

Just sit comfortably for a moment. Close your eyes. Think of someone who was helpful to you in a time of trouble. See that person in your mind. Send that person your feelings of gratitude and love. See that person smile in response. Feel the sensation of total relaxation course through your body and mind.

Whenever you feel sad or depressed, down and out, remember to take a few moments to extend gratitude to those you love, and to those who have helped you along the path of life. Your focus will change and you will get up feeling happier, healthier, and more alive.

Do something

▪ ARLO GUTHRIE

Ask a twenty-five-year-old if she's ever heard of Arlo Guthrie and her "Who's that?" makes one realize that a definite generation gap exists. To a fifty-six-year-old, it seems obvious that everyone should have seen Guthrie perform on a VH-1 or MTV Woodstock (the original) retrospective. For the boomer generation, once known as hippies or flower children, Arlo Guthrie was a symbol of their "make love, not war" worldview.

Guthrie grew up in a musical family. His father was folk singer Woody Guthrie, whose songs inspired and uplifted the depression-plagued country during the 1930s. His mother, Marjorie, was a professional dancer with the Martha Graham Company.

Arlo Guthrie was made famous by the 1967 song "Alice's Restaurant Massacree," which tells the long, very funny, tale of Guthrie's arrest for littering which eventually gets him out of going into the army. The song was made into a movie in 1969. That same year, Guthrie appeared at the Woodstock concert and in the subsequent movie. His pronouncement that "The New York State Thruway is closed, man," captured the power and potential of a generation that thought it would change the world.

These days, Guthrie is an entertainer, businessman, spiritual devotee and dedicated social activist. As an entertainer, he tours the globe ten months out of the year. As a businessman, he is the founder of Rising Son Records, a production company that books all his concerts and distributes his many CD's. As a spiritual devotee, he is committed to supporting the work of Ma Jaya Sati Bhagavati. To Guthrie, spiritual living means being a social activist and doing something to make a positive difference in the world. He has opened the Guthrie Center in Massachusetts, which is an inter-faith spiritual community that provides outreach services to the sick and poor both locally and globally.

Arlo's humor, irreverence, and activism found in his music have also been a part of his spiritual journey, which he shares below.

I got into spirituality because of food. I was in love with Indian food and there were no Indian restaurants at all when I went to Los Angeles in 1966. I had come from New York where there was a large Indian community. Suddenly, I go out to California and there's nothing. The only place you could get Indian food was at this guy Yogananda's place. I didn't know anything about him. All I knew was that he was some kind of Swami guy. The place was an ashram, a center, and if you were a member, you could get a bowl of curry for 35 cents. Non-members had to pay $1.35. So, because I was broke in those days, I joined to get cheap food.

Because I was a member, they started sending me their lit-erature every week. I thought, "Since I already paid for it, why don't I read it to see what the story is?" So I read Yogananda's book, *Autobiography of a Yogi,* and loved him. I thought he was a beautiful guy. I didn't know anything about this stuff. We were all listening to Beatles tunes with sitars and things, but I didn't know anything much beyond that. As part of the weekly material, they sent yoga breathing exercises and a week's worth of instructions in the Yogananda course. But after being on the road for six months, I'd come home to find a 3-foot pile of Yogananda literature. So I stayed with the breathing and found that whenever I was in trouble, all I had to do was sit down and do this breathing. Pretty soon I'd feel good. I've done this all my life since then.

I was always interested in God. I wanted to know, "What's the story; what's the truth?" I was always interested in who we are without all of the trappings. If you take away all the cars and the kitchens, if you take away all the bathrooms, if you take away all the stuff, who are you really? These kinds of thoughts interested me as they did an entire generation. We used to call it getting back to nature, but the truth was we were just trying to figure out who we were in relation to an ever-changing world. We were trying to figure out what it is about being a human being that is really part of being a human being—and what is part of being in a world filled with all kinds of gadgets.

Drugs, like so many other things, helped us escape the traditional confines of culture because there was a point at which my generation realized that if we continue to do things the same way as our parents, we would end up at this place where we would be using weapons of mass destruction to the point that there might not be a world anymore. All of these traditional values that everyone still espouses today had brought us to the brink of a global disaster. They brought us to that point, not only in theory, but in fact, since we had used them already. The question was whether we would use them again. My generation said, "We can't do that. We cannot continue in the same way." So we threw out all the distinctions between us: economic, religious, social, and educational. We said, "To hell with that; let's see who we really are. Who are we without the soap? Who are we without the diplomas? Who are we without the educational system?"

Thirty years ago civil rights, women's rights, clean water, clean air, no nukes, education, were so controversial they weren't even talked about. These issues have become normal everyday American ideas that people talk about and debate. That is what it should have been like in 1969, which is why you saw so many people on the streets. Now we see millions of people all over the world take to the streets right before the Iraq war to have their opinion—whether for it or against it—heard. They wanted to have their voices counted and they believed that someone would actually listen. It took 10 years to get to that place in 1969. It took two weeks to get to that place in 2003.

Ma Jaya Sati Bhagavati was the first spiritual teacher I met who didn't need translating. All the other great thinkers and teachers I read or met had a kind of mystery to them in some way. They didn't talk my language. But Ma comes from a few streets away from where I grew up in Coney Island in Brooklyn, New York. Not only was Ma speaking my language, but she was speaking from her heart, and I fell in love with her, not just for her teaching. I'm interested in the teaching; I find it all fascinating. More importantly, I grew up in a family that was convinced that you could do whatever you want—but if, in addition, you didn't do something to make a difference in the world, you were just wasting everybody's time. And Ma did things. I found a person whose work I knew was important regardless of her teaching; regardless of whether she was a guru or not. I would support her to the end of the world, just because of what she does.

When I opened the Guthrie Center, I thought, in a humble way, that we might be able to continue some little bit of what Ma Jaya did at Kashi Ashram as an offshoot. Ma's basic philosophy is to be kind. It sounds simple, but it's probably the most important thing in the world right now. I thought: How does somebody learn to be kind? It has to be learned. You might be born with it, but it gets lost somewhere. So we started our organization to follow in the way of kindness.

There are a lot of organizations whose credo is, "Do it our way and the world will be great." We wanted to form an organization that would respond to the needs of the community on both a local and a global level. To that end we went with Ma to South Africa a few years ago as part of our global effort. We started a school for kids.

My dad died of Huntington's disease, which is a degenerative nerve disease that you inherit from your parents. And so at an early age, I knew that if I were to do something, I had to do it quick. There was a 50-50 shot that I would come down with the same thing, and I knew I couldn't take a chance. My father went into the hospital when he was in his forties. So I thought that before I was in my forties, I better do what I want to do. Then if I lived past that age, and I didn't get the disease, I would have some free time. So now, I have free time, and in my free time I started the church and the organizations that go with it. I continue to support Ma and I continue to sing my songs and live my life. Since I'm living on free time now, my life is a holiday.

for reflection

Arlo Guthrie thinks the most important thing in the world right now is to be kind. The difference between kindness and courtesy is an obvious one. When you are courteous you expect people to react in kind, expecting them to be courteous to you, too, and to have good manners, and do the expected thing.

An act of kindness is different. An act of kindness expects no response whatsoever. An act of kindness is completely impersonal without judgment or reservation. An act of kindness is a blessing.

There are two ways to be kind. First, is the inner way. Just the idea of visualizing people in your mind, and finding one kind thought by which to characterize them will actually have an effect. Some people have tried this mental exercise, and found that hostile people became friendly without knowing why. Mental acts of kindness communicate and no one understands exactly how or why.

The second way to be kind takes a physical act. Loving touches, a smile, an offered hand, a nod of greeting, or even respectful recognition are simple things anyone can do easily.

The most important act of kindness I received in my lifetime was a gift of a $5 bill given to me by a perfect stranger when I was in dire financial need. I asked for his address so that I could repay him. "No! No," he said, "I want you to pass it on."

Whenever someone wants to repay me for some favor or other, I tell the story of the $5 bill and ask them to pass the favor on. So, think about it for a moment: has anyone ever helped you in time of need? Have you passed it on?

Following the spiritual impulse

■ NATHAN KATZ, PH.D.

Dr. Nathan Katz has his finger on South Florida's spiritual pulse. As chair for the past nine years of Florida International University's Religious Studies Department, Katz's mission is to represent the breadth of South Florida's spiritual traditions. "In Miami we're interested in diaspora traditions," Katz reflects. "We have Caribbean, African, Jewish, Muslim, and Asian traditions mingling with fervent Protestantism and charismatic Catholicism. We also have a great many people involved in the so-called secular spiritualities or "New Age" movement and in the women's movement. There are also a number of Native traditions. It's all right here. People have come here from all over the world."

Nathan's own life reflects an intimate familiarity with religious diversity. He was one of a delegation of Jewish leaders that traveled to India for a dialog with the Dalai Lama. The Dalai Lama wanted to know why Judaism was still thriving despite thousands of years of diaspora. Nathan served as translator for the group. He was the perfect choice for the task since he speaks Tibetan fluently. He had spent several years in the Middle East and India studying Buddhism and Hinduism. Ironically, it was the time he spent living in a Jewish community in the town of Cochin in southern India that caused him to embrace Orthodox Judaism as his primary spiritual practice. Nathan wrote about his India experiences in his book *Who Are the Jews of India?*

I was born into a traditional Jewish family in Camden, New Jersey. At the age of five, I announced to my family, during a Shabbat dinner, that I was going to go to India. Fifteen years later, I did.

My first trip to India was in 1969. I was shocked and horrified, as many people are on their first trip, by the overwhelming smells and dirt and number of beggars. The trip put me in touch with some experiences that were unexplainable, but somehow I knew that the esoteric traditions would provide meaning to those experiences. Upon return to the States, I went into Jungian therapy which provided a framework for understanding those experiences. I also read the Evan-Wentz edition of *The Tibetan Book of the Dead*, which was one of the important moments in my life. Nothing excited me as much. I knew I had to read it in the original. I had to know what it said. I decided to study the Tibetan language as well as classical Sanskrit.

The spiritual impulse that had always been part of my life was piqued by experimentation with drugs, like so many of my 1960s contemporaries. I'd be dishonest to say that my experience with psychedelics wasn't a part of my spiritual awakening. It gave me a glimpse of where I was trying to go. I'm not sure that it got me any closer, but, at least it gave me a sense that there was a place to go.

After college, I worked for the U.S. Information Agency in Afghanistan. I learned the language and studied Islam at the local university. My spiritual hunger was fed through study with Sufi masters living in the mountains, and for a while, I embraced the Sufi tradition. When my service was up, I went to India and spent a year studying with Hindu and Buddhist teachers. Years later, after receiving a Ph.D. in Indology, the study of classical India, I went on sabbatical and, with my wife, visited the ancient Jewish community of Cochin located in southern India. We wanted to memorialize the community in a book and two years later we went back to do just that. We spent a year doing participant/observer field work with that community and it caught us totally unawares. We found that after spending a year living in a Sephardic Jewish home and immersing ourselves in the rhythm of the community—me, praying every day with the men in the synagogue—by the time we left, it was in our blood. I realized that what I thought was a professional, anthropological interest had turned back on me and changed me. While I still do some scholarship in Buddhism and Hinduism, now I do Indo-Judaic studies. But my life as an orthodox Jew is still informed by Hindu and Buddhist friends and texts.

Spirituality is rooted in religious traditions. There are religious traditions that have spiritual or esoteric components. These days, many people are disenchanted with religious institutions, yet remain drawn to the spiritual wisdom that they contain. So you have an interesting phenomenon of the secularization of spirituality, which usually comes through various kinds of healing techniques. These can be transpersonal psychology or energy work, those kinds of things. If I wanted to be cynical about it, I would say that people, who want spirituality, don't want to pay their dues to the church or synagogue.

But it's not that simple. Often people have good reasons to be alienated from institutional religions, yet they seek what is at the heart of religion. It's interesting, too, that students are finding the university as a substitute. It's a new kind of secular/spiritual path for them. I find that students in my classes are there because they are looking for something, but are shut off in their churches, synagogues.

In my everyday life, I practice *Vipassana,* or mindfulness meditation, that I learned in Sri Lanka to help with daily stressors that are a part of every day life. When driving on route 836 every morning and some guy cuts me off, I watch myself get angry. I feel the anger. I watch the anger dissipate. That's mindfulness. Vipassana or mindfulness is observing the mind and the emotions. It's a tremendous skill. You just don't engage your ego and thoughts and emotions, you just watch them. It's not "I am angry;" it's "there's anger right now."

Not everyone has a spiritual impulse; some people are interested and some people aren't. It's like anything else. But, if someone feels the spark, he or she doesn't have to go anywhere to find the truth. It's all within you, however you understand it: within you, among us, up there, down here. Wherever it is, it's where you are. In a metaphysical or deeper sense, you never have to go anywhere to find it. One can find truth everywhere. Truth is universal.

for reflection

Dr. Katz talks about the spiritual impulse that is in each and every one of us. He talks of the traditional paths to spirituality and New Age disciplines and other nontraditional paths one might explore.

A good idea for students on the path of spirituality would be to explore different religions, philosophies, and other nontraditional ways of identifying with the power that is within and without, shared by every one of us ... the way to peace, love, and understanding.

If you find yourself able to resonate with a religion, a discipline, a tradition, a way of being in the world but not of it, you will have found your way home. You will have found a way to relate to the universe so that unease, despair, fear and hate and anger can no longer control your psyche, because you have seen the light, you have experienced peace of mind.

Walking the talk

■ JUDITH LIGHT

Actress Judith Light is known for her many years as Angela Bower on TV's *Who's the Boss?* She has a recurring role as district attorney on *Law and Order, Special Victim's Unit.* A star of stage as well as television, Judith mesmerized audiences playing Dr. Vivian Bearing, a college professor who was dying of ovarian cancer, in the play *Wit.* The role required Judith to shave her head. She not only shaved her head, but appeared bald on television talk shows, and in newspaper and magazine photographs.

An advocate for AIDS awareness, Judith has been a student of consciousness since the early days of Werner Erhardt's est training. Under the tutelage of her manager, Herb Hamsher, she has explored paths of enlightenment and spirituality. However, her main goal is to embody the teachings, not just pay lip service to them. In a profession that can promote egotism and self-aggrandizement, Judith works at relinquishing her ego so that she can be used as a spiritual instrument unconditionally.

I don't know what my purpose is. I just keep doing what's in front of me. I mean, God, or whatever you want to call the universal force, really knows what the purpose is. But I don't think it's for me to know what it is. I do what's in front of me, what's presented to me, to the best of my ability. And I just sort of get out of the way. A lot of times I get in the way, and I don't do what is presented to me. I'm too much in my ego. But trying to say what my purpose is sounds kind of arrogant or too lofty. I don't think of it like that. You know, it's like the George Bernard Shaw quote: "Life is no brief candle to me. It is a sort of splendid torch which I have got a hold of for the moment, and I want to make it burn as brightly as possible before handing it on to future generations."

I just look and see what there is for me to do, and I try to get out of the way enough to do it. When I started getting involved in AIDS causes, I began to see the real issue underlying what was happening in relation to people getting taken care of and people getting support: it was the fact that there was so much homophobia in this country. The next natural thing for me to get involved in was human rights. Now I'm playing a woman with cancer in the play *Wit* and cancer becomes the next thing I get involved in. That's how it works for me; I see what's there to do and do it.

I shaved my head for my role in *Wit*. I can say that I am using this as a way to focus on myself so that I can feel beautiful inside without my hair; that it wasn't my hair that made me beautiful. But I don't trust myself because it's paradoxical. I also know that my going without my wig is, to a degree, so that I can empathize with people who have lost their hair due to chemotherapy, baldness gene, or alopecia. I can say I want to show my solidarity with them. But I also know that programming is very tricky, because there is a way in which it makes me look brave and courageous and invites people to put me on a pedestal for doing it. That's really dicey for me. So I have to be very vigilant. I'm not saying that it wasn't brave. I'm not saying that it isn't a valuable lesson to use and to go after, but am I there yet? I can't tell you the truth about that. I don't know, because I still feel the pull of my ego.

Sometimes I feel, "Oh, yes, I must do this because it will save the world and contribute to the world in a major way." That's my ego. That is absolutely without question my ego. If I'm talking about saving the world, that means I'm not focusing on the issues that I have to deal with within myself. And those are the only things that I can handle.

In the est training, Werner Erhardt talked about the paradigm that we have to follow: when your being comes first, then you know what to do. Then you will have a result. But it's never about the result. It's about the process; it's about the journey. When I met my manager, Herb Hamsher, I said, "I would like to be able to grow. I want to be able to use my career and give back in some way." He said, "Well, I can help you do that. I cannot promise you that it will be easy, but I can promise you that it will be alive." So growth has always been my context. This has required a tremendous amount of physical, emotional, psychological, and spiritual effort on my part.

I have to work at faith; it isn't something I just wake up in the morning and have. I have to discipline myself to it. I work to see that the glass is half full, as opposed to half empty. That's why I worry about the things I say and the way I say them: I worry about the way they come across. New Age stuff can be a defense against actually doing anything. I know that's been so for me. When I'm not careful, I can read every book and quote everything, and still be stuck in the same place. Movement is very important to me. We're here to get ourselves up to another level. In fact, *A Course in Miracles* says that if one person is healed, the rest of the world will be healed.

I just keep working on what I see is necessary for me to do and do not get defensive when I get input. Herb Hamsher says we're not able to see all sides of ourselves. We don't have eyes in the back of our heads, but two people hugging each other have 360-degree vision. We need someone outside our system who can tell us what they see in us and what we're doing that isn't working. It's essential to listen to that. It's work. Some days I can do it, and some days I can't.

I want to be beyond where I am, but I'm not, and it's essential for me to say that I am where I am. You can only understand life looking backward, but you have to live it going forward. That's one of the things that Herb talks about all the time. Herb is a remarkable person. He really lives what he talks about. I see it because I'm around him all the time. He's very human. At the same time, he is always working on himself so that he can be as clear as possible.

What I want to do is to be inspired by people who are living and transforming their lives without having cancer, getting AIDS, or anything else. I think our purpose is to make a choice to transform.

Transformation is to choose to put yourself through something that you don't think you want or that makes you uncomfortable. In other words, to choose your own growth is to choose the road less traveled.

for reflection

Judith Light talks about purpose, growth and transformation. She is not at all sure about her purpose, or transformation, but she is sure about the concept of growth. She is committed to growth. She feels her purpose will become very clear and transformation will be inevitable as long as she focuses on growth

Many of us today see purpose in life as ever-shifting, like the sand dunes pushed from one location to another by the winds in the Sahara desert. Purpose seems to change from one situation to another. Transformation is an inevitable consequence of growth. Transformation cannot be predicted, it is part of the future, but growth is in the present; it is in the now, and can be focused on to great effect.

Just how do we focus on growth? In order to grow consciously we first must accept exactly where we are; then, we set a goal. The goal must be realistic and simple. For example if I am a typist, who is competent at typing 15 words per minute without error, then I can set a realistic goal for myself to become competent at typing 20 words per minute without error within three months. I can create a daily schedule with a practice time of 30 minutes per day. The probability, if I can keep to the discipline of the schedule, will be that I will be successful. The lesson is to start with a very simple goal for growth. Many people set goals for growth that are unrealistic and unattainable. They program themselves for failure.

Think of your own situation. Choose an area in which you wish to grow. What is your present competency in this area? Can you create a realistic goal for growth? What discipline will you need to maintain in order to reach this goal? If you can answer these questions competently, your growth is assured.

Being a spiritual man

∎ TOBY THOMPKINS

Toby Thompkins is a *mensch*. That's a Yiddish word for a righteous person. But Toby is more than just righteous: He is a visionary. Toby's vision is a world were all people are seen as one, where all people are treated with dignity and respect, and where all people are afforded the same opportunities. Toby believes that human differences can be used as a lesson plan for healing. Toby's work as a corporate consultant in the areas of leadership and diversity, have given him an opportunity to make his vision manifest. His first book, *The Real Lives of Strong Black Women: Transcending Myths, Reclaiming Joy*, hits a universal tone that cuts across races and religions.

To Toby, living spiritually is about discovering the fullness of his humanity. At forty-three, through his many years of in-depth spiritual study, he understands what it means to be a spiritual being having a human experience.

Something happened to me when I entered my forties; I began to look more deeply at the things in life that I had taken for granted. After four decades of walking around on the planet, upon a closer examination of my inner life, I began to realize that many of the givens I had blindly incorporated into my way of being were simply not being supported. My self-examination centered on what it means to be a man, what it means to be a Black man, what it means to be a good man, and what it means to be human. As I probed my inner world and evaluated my daily experiences, I realized that I needed to rethink myself as a whole being. I realized that the sovereignty that we seek as men is difficult to experience when it is the subset of the comparative agendas of gender, race, class, or even morality. What I was searching for was beyond the attainment of the greener grass side of the fence, and it surpassed those honorable positions we strive for in life of being the first, the best, or the only. Over time, I have come to see that we are all striving to know ourselves beyond these uniquely human forms of comparative identity. Over time, I have come to believe that doing so is the only way to ensure our individual and collective growth and protect our survival.

To become whole is to be fully self-expressed as a spiritual being. In doing so, men encounter a daily struggle to divest ourselves from the shared agenda of masculinity and invest ourselves in the higher agenda of humanity. If men are willing to do the rigorous work of self-examination, the rich and diverse combinations of human traits, conditions, and characteristics through which we define our separateness as men, will begin to inform our relatedness as spiritual beings.

In my forty-three years as a Black man in America, I have been a student of many religious philosophies. Each one advocates a unique position about what it means to be a man and each one has brought me a little closer to a deeper understanding of who I am as a spiritual being. But the greatest teacher in my life has not been the framework of one religion over another. Rather, it has been my observation of and participation in those powerful unplanned moments in life when men and mankind are called together as one by the power of love.

During these moments in life, I am reminded of the under-utilized capacity of the spirit in the everyday lives of men. Why are men most likely to comfort, nurture, and heal the less fortunate in times of natural disaster or national tragedy? Why can't we choose to be that vulnerable to the well-being of our fellow man each and every day? To be fully self-expressed as a spiritual being is to be vulnerable, open, and affected. Yet for many of the men I talk to, to be vulnerable is to be weak, to be a failure, and to be less than a man.

Vulnerability is a great teacher. In actuality to be vulnerable is not to be weak. It is to come to know yourself through your relationship with something that is greater than you. I strive to stay vulnerable to the notion that I am a spiritual being having a human experience. Through this state of vulnerability I can embrace the wisdom and divine logic of my spiritual reality. Through vulnerability I can call forth a compassion that transcends my manhood and invokes a greater compassion for the spiritual being that resides in every human being. To me, what it means to be a man is to honor all humans.

for reflection

Toby Thompkins tells us that to be fully self-expressed as a spiritual being is to be vulnerable, open, and affected.

There have been many situations in our lives where we have responded fearfully, defensively and perhaps angrily to a happening that might have been healed if we had the courage to be vulnerable and open.

Try this simple exercise.

Make yourself comfortable in your chair. Take a few deep breaths, and close your eyes. Relax. Relax. Relax. Remember a time when you missed an opportunity to be open, helpful, and loving, and instead acted fearfully and defensively. Visualize curtains parting to reveal a bright movie screen. Play that situation on the movie screen of your mind. See situation unfold from the beginning to the end, and feel the pangs of regret of a missed opportunity to be open and loving.

Replay this scene in your mind. This time, change the script. See yourself as courageous enough to become vulnerable and courageous enough to extend love and healing instead of fear and defensiveness. Play this scene again. Congratulations. You have just changed your mind. The human mind can not tell the difference between a real experience and a vicarious or imaginary one. If you did this exercise honestly, then you can be assured that the imaginary experience you just underwent will condition your mind to act very differently when a similar situation calls forth some kind of response from you. Be assured that you will not react out of fear and defensiveness. You have now programmed your mind to act with love and compassion.

Nurturing the spiritual spark

■ DAN WAKEFIELD

Dan Wakefield's career as a novelist, journalist, and screenwriter spans nearly five decades. In addition to best-selling novels *Going All the Way* and *Starting Over,* which were produced as feature films, he created the NBC primetime TV series *James at 15.* In addition, a documentary film has been produced of his memoir *New York in the Fifties.*

Dan describes himself as a non-recruiting Christian and believes that people's actions define their spirituality. Even during Wakefield's atheist years, he was inspired by and wrote about people who modeled compassion. Among his influences is Dorothy Day, who started the Catholic Worker Movement in New York City. Day lived on the Bowery, home to many of the city's population of derelicts. Day fed and helped clothe whoever needed it. Another influence on his spiritual belief system was the people who started the East Harlem Protestant Parish. They raised and nurtured children in what was one of the worst slums in New York City. Dan has shared his own spiritual journey, and has helped thousands of people to tap into their own spiritual impulse through his many spiritually-themed books including *Returning: A Spiritual Journey* and *The Story of Your Life: Writing a Spiritual Autobiography.* Dan is currently Writer in Residence at Florida International University. For Dan, there are two essentials of spiritual living: one is being part of a spiritual community, and the other, perhaps even more important, is seeing the world through the eyes of his goddaughter.

There's a quote I have on my website from an ancient sage that says, "Be kind, for everyone you meet is fighting a great battle." I feel that if we could keep that in mind, it would help us not to get angry at people or put them down. It's helpful to me when I remember that everyone has problems, battles, decisions, and other challenges that make us human beings. About eight years ago, something unexpected happened that has enriched my life. I met a family that had a little girl who is now nine years old, and the mother asked me to have her daughter baptized since they didn't go to any church. I did. And then I started taking her to Sunday school, and she's become the biggest part of my life. The greatest part of my spiritual life has been being with her and listening to her.

We have a ritual of walking around a few blocks where she lives, and she sees things that I don't see. I remember once we stopped because she saw some snails. She wanted to hold the snails in her hand. She was so patient while she held a snail in her hand, and eventually it came out of its shell. That was really funny, because I remembered listening to a speaker talk about a book in which somebody had gone to India to study with famous religious gurus: he had learned to be quiet and to watch a spider creating a web. He learned to watch nature with patience. And I started laughing because I didn't have to go to Asia to learn that lesson; I just had to go around the block with my goddaughter.

My experience has been that when I go to some far-off place that advertises itself to be spiritual, it always turns out to be a bust. I once went to the Island of Iona. Several people who had been there told me I had to go, because you just feel "these spiritual vibes." And when I went there it rained day and night. I had nightmares. Then I was told that the place was sometimes haunted by one of the early saints who had lived there.

I've always found meaning right where I live and with whomever I know. I went back to church in 1980 and became a member of a church in Boston named King's Chapel, which became a major part of my life. I feel that I've been led to places like that, and I appreciate it very deeply. I think that there's a way you can be a spiritual person all on your own and meditate and pray by yourself. But for me, being part of a worshipping community adds another dimension to my spiritual life, whatever that community is: Buddhist, Jewish, Hindu, or Muslim. Simply being with other people who are also seekers and who are involved in the same quest you are is very meaningful.

I think there should not be a difference between being religious and being spiritual, but sometimes there is; when I go to my church and I see the people and take part in the activities, I feel that it's spiritual. It's not something that's cordoned off into the category of "religion." For me it doesn't matter what you call it. Whatever is genuine and nurturing; some people are put off by organized religion, and they call it spirituality. And I think there are some churches where people go on Sunday morning and do their duty; that's sort of a hollow kind of religion. But I also think there are many people who go to church and are nurtured and nourished.

As a child I was very involved in the church. I was baptized on my own volition when I was eleven years old. I sought out a church and I wanted to be baptized. When I went back to church, I was at a low point in my life. After reading a lot and talking to a lot of people over the years, I understand that it is common for people to return to religion or seek it out when they are at a low point in their lives or at a very high point in their lives. An example of a high point would be Tolstoy who, when he became acknowledged as the greatest novelist in Russia and maybe the world, was dealing with, "Is that all there is? Shouldn't I be feeling more than this?" The hollowness of worldly success turned him to religion. But for most seekers, like me, it occurs at a low point.

I had just spent difficult years in Hollywood. I was drinking too much. I had a pulse of 120. I was in very bad health. I went back to Boston and got into an exercise and diet program and lost 20 pounds. My pulse went down to 80, but they said it should be 60. They asked me if I would be willing to go a month without a drinking. It was something I had never done before in my adult life, but I did. It was during that time that I had an impulse to go to church on Christmas Eve. I always thought that it was no accident that when my mind was clear—meaning when I wasn't numbing myself with anything—that I experienced a spiritual impulse. A lot of times alcohol and drugs really numb the spiritual impulse, and if you stop and change your lifestyle to get more clarity, one of the first things that comes up is some wish for some kind connection to spirituality. That's what happened to me.

for reflection

Dan Wakefield talks about the spiritual impulse that, when activated, causes an attitudinal change that opens up the font of inspiration hidden deep inside of all of us.

There are many ways to access our hidden inspiration. One way is to join a group of people who gather together for spiritual or religious purposes. You'll find, just as Dan Wakefield found, that being with people in that setting can make us aware of our own inspiration and delight in life.

For many people individual prayer and meditation opens the gates to spiritual inspiration. For other people, studying the writings of saints, gurus and enlightened masters whose words touch their heart is another way to allow your inspiration to flow.

How do you find your spiritual impulse? There is no right or wrong way. All that's needed is an authentic yearning for connection to something larger than yourself. If sharing that experience with others nurtures your soul, then do that. If seeking that connection in solitude brings you peace, then spend time doing that. For some people, the practices of yoga or tai chi are particularly effective ways of connecting to their spiritual impulse.

If you like, you can make that connection in a sincere request for peace by taking a few deep breaths and just suspending time. Just by taking a few moments to dispel your mind's activity and focus on your breath, can remind you of your connection to whatever you want to call the totality of all that is.

manifesting
your dreams

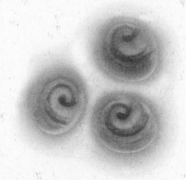

Consciousness and money

■ MARC ALLEN

Marc Allen is so nice and so kind that it is hard to imagine that he's made millions of dollars in business. His philosophy is simple and it works: you manifest what you focus on.

In addition to being a successful businessman—he's the founder, along with Shakti Gawain, of New World Library—Marc is an author and composer. His books include *Visionary Business: An Entrepreneur's Guide to Success,* and *The Millionaire Course.* His albums include *Breathe, Petals,* and *Solo Flight.* He is also a popular inspirational speaker. His passion is infectious.

Marc has studied both Zen and Tibetan Buddhism with renowned masters. His path has included living in "back-to-the-land" and spiritual communities. In the essay below, he recounts the transformation that occurred when he was thirty years old. The tools he used to turn his life around form the foundation of his teachings. His primary teaching is that success can be acquired in a healthy, positive way. Marc does not distinguish between his business life and his spiritual life. He applies spiritual practices such as praying and tithing to his business life. He teaches the importance of creating partnerships with co-workers, employees, and business associates.

In his essay, Marc shares the simple tools he used that brought him material as well as spiritual wealth.

The day I turned thirty, I decided to start a publishing company. I had no knowledge of business in general or publishing in particular. I had no money, no rich friends, no relatives with any cash to spare. I had no job, no income, and no assets. I had been an actor until our company fell apart. Then I was a musician until our band fell apart. Then I turned thirty, and went into shock. I wasn't a kid anymore.

I spent much of the day pacing in my little studio apartment in the slums of Oakland, California. It slowly dawned on me that I had no direction in life, no goals whatsoever, except scrounging up enough money for my morning latte and my rent. Then I remembered a little game I had played one time, years before, during a failed back-to-the-land experiment. The game simply involved imagining that five years had passed and everything had gone as well as you could possibly imagine. What would your life look like? What is your "ideal scene"?

As soon as I asked myself the question, what felt at the time like a vast, unobtainable vision sprang to mind: I owned a successful publishing company that published my books as well as those of others, yet I still had time for playing and recording my music as well as having lots of quiet time to myself. I had an easy and relaxed lifestyle and I owned a big white house on a hill in Marin County, one of the most beautiful places on earth.

As soon as I had that vision of the future, my doubts and fears rushed in, powerful and overwhelming. I soon realized that the most important work for me to do was the inner work necessary to overcome those doubts and fears. I had my work cut out for me. It took years to learn to trust myself, and years of affirming I was now creating success in an easy and relaxed manner, in a healthy and positive way—but eventually I overcame a great many of my doubts and fears. Once that happened, my ideal scene began to be realized. It took me ten years, but I have now achieved everything I dreamed of the day I turned thirty.

A visionary plan

Over the years I developed a simple system that I teach in workshops and in my book, *The Millionaire Course: A Visionary Plan for Creating the Life of Your Dreams*. It all goes back to the basic steps I discovered on my thirtieth birthday:

First write your ideal scene. If everything went as well as you could possibly imagine, what would your life look like? Put it on paper—there is a power that comes into play as soon as we commit our ideas to paper.

Then take another sheet of paper and list all of your major goals that are embedded in your ideal scene. I had twelve goals when I first did it; now I have seven. Just list them, in writing: establish a successful business, for example. Then rewrite each goal, on another sheet of paper, as an affirmation.

The wording of a successful affirmation can be tricky, because it should be stated in the present tense, yet it should be believable to your conscious and subconscious mind. If you write "I am now a millionaire," and in reality you're scrounging to pay the rent, your mind won't accept the affirmation. But if you write "I am now becoming financially successful," that's something your mind can accept. That's a good affirmation.

For years, this was one of my affirmations: *I am sensible and in control of my finances. I am creating total financial success, in an easy and relaxed manner, in a healthy and positive way.* That affirmation proved very powerful for me. Read and repeat your list of affirmations several times a week. Once you do, you'll be led to the next step: making a plan for every major goal. At first you may not have any idea of what the plan might be to achieve financial independence or start a successful business or have a fulfilling relationship. But once you start affirming it, the first few steps to take will become obvious.

Eventually, a plan will form in your mind. When it does, write it down. Keep it short, just a page or two. For some goals, you may need a longer plan, but for every goal, develop a short, one-page plan with the goal at the top and the strategies for achieving that goal listed down the page.

Put all of this in a folder, and refer to it often. The single most powerful tool I have for creating success is my folder that contains my ideal scene, goals, goals listed as affirmations, and single-page plans for every major goal.

For each goal, you can develop not just one strategy to achieve it, but a multi-pronged strategy: First you try this, if that doesn't work you try something else. If that doesn't work, you do something else entirely. A multi-pronged strategy refuses to take "no" for an answer.

Consciousness and money

When I was thirty I was a poverty case. When I was thirty-five, I was $65,000 in credit-card debt and on the brink of bankruptcy. By the time I was forty, I was a millionaire, several times over. What changed in those five years?

Nothing out there in the outer world changed; there were no more or no fewer opportunities or problems. The only thing that changed was within my mind, in my thought processes. I learned how to go beyond my limiting poverty consciousness and move into a much more expansive state of mind.

I learned how to become aware of my deep core beliefs, and realized I had a conflicting mass of beliefs, many of them negative and limiting. I believed life is a struggle, it's hard to succeed, money doesn't grow on trees, and money corrupts. I learned something about our beliefs: They are not true in themselves, but if we believe them, they become true in our experience.

I grew to realize a lot of other people have a very different set of beliefs than I do and, best of all, I found I can change my beliefs. It's not that difficult, but it does take work. First of all, we have to become conscious of our beliefs. Then we have to consciously change them. The process requires becoming aware of every thought we have, at every moment. Once we can do that, we can change our habitual thinking.

I looked at it as literally reprogramming my mind. When I would think, "This is really hard, this is a big problem," I would catch myself thinking that and insert a new program. I would think, "In an easy and relaxed manner, in a healthy and positive way, I see opportunities everywhere," or something else that would contradict the old negative programming.

Take a look at your deep core beliefs. They are reflected in your thoughts, words, and actions. These kind of questions can get to the root of things: Do you believe life is a struggle? Do you believe there is a scarcity of money, time, or energy? Do you believe it's really hard to succeed? Do you believe deep down that you're lacking some crucial ingredient for success?

I have come to see and believe that once we set our endlessly creative minds in the right direction, there are no obstacles that can't be overcome. And setting this direction is simply a matter of focusing on our goals, affirming them, making a plan, and taking the first obvious steps.

All the other things we thought were essential for success don't matter. You don't need money. You don't need a lot of intelligence. You don't need experience. You don't need a college education. All you need to do is focus your mind on your goal, and ask your creative subconscious mind what the next steps are that you need to take toward the goal.

That's the secret of success, in a nutshell: Have a clear goal in mind and persist. James Allen put it this way in *As You Think,* one of my favorite inspirational books:

"You will become as great as your dominant aspiration. If you cherish a vision, a lofty ideal in your heart, you will realize it."

for reflection

Try the following exercise that Marc Allen suggested in his essay.

Visualize what you want to create in your life, whether it's an ideal job, relationship, home, health, or whatever you wish.

Write down your vision on a piece of paper.

On a second sheet of paper, write all the major goals that creating that ideal scene requires.

On a separate piece of paper, rewrite your goals as an affirmations.

Write your affirmations in the present tense. Make them believable to your own mind.

Read and repeat your affirmations several times a week.

As you do this, you will be led to your next step and a plan to achieve your goals will take form.

When your plan for achieving each of your goals forms, write down your plan for achieving each goal.

Keep everything you wrote in a folder.

Reread your ideal scene, goals, goals listed as affirmations, and single-page plans for every major goal as often as possible.

As you do this, new ways for achieving your goals will come to you. Keep taking the most obvious steps in front of you and prepare yourself for some truly marvelous results.

Making our dreams come true

■ JACK CANFIELD

Jack Canfield and business partner Mark Victor Hansen are the creators of the *Chicken Soup for the Soul*® empire. To date, forty million *Chicken Soup* books have been published under eighteen different titles. There are *Chicken Soup* books for teenagers, couples, women, kids, and just about anyone else you can think of. Jack's latest book is *The Success Principles: How to Get from Where You Are to Where You Want to Be.*™

Jack teaches what he calls "the principles of effective living." These include communication skills, self-awareness skills, self-esteem, conflict management, value clarification, problem solving, and goal setting.

He has always been altruistically motivated. As a small boy, he wanted to be a lawyer and handle pro bono cases for the poor. Recognizing that he did not have the adversarial nature required to be a lawyer, Jack turned to teaching as a career. Teaching quenched his altruistic thirst to make a positive contribution to his country. He taught in inner city schools and became head of a Job Corps program. Eventually, he took his experiences of motivating those who did not want to learn into the corporate arena. His mission became "inspiring and empowering people to live their highest vision in the context of love and joy." That mission applies to the classroom as well as to corporate boardrooms.

To Jack, spiritual living means right livelihood—to live one's dreams in such a way as to not harm others, and to make a positive contribution to the world.

I don't think most Americans are living their dreams. I think most Americans, Canadians, and the people in what I call the "developed nations" are leading lives that are comfortable to a certain extent, but they aren't really living their dreams. The reason they're not doing it is because they're living in quiet resignation. It's scary. They have to pay their bills, but they're not really satisfied in their jobs. They're afraid to take the risk to go back to school, to learn a new trade or profession, to start their own business, to become a consultant—whatever their dream is. I'll tell you, when people take my workshops, within a year at least 50% of them are doing something different than what they were doing the year before. They may still be at the same company, but they're doing a different job, or doing it in a different way. Many people quit their jobs and start their own businesses, poetry magazines, retreat centers, and so forth.

People who aren't satisfied with their lives are usually blamers and complainers. They blame the world for how it is and complain, "It's not my fault. They did it to me." I'm not saying it's even true we're 100% responsible for our lives. I'm saying act as if we are. What we found in the research is that people who act as if they are 100% responsible for their lives start solving the things that need to be solved. They say, "Here I am. Where do I want to be? No one else can take me there. What do I have to do to get there? What about my current situation that I'm creating could I stop creating?" You have to take this position: the way the world is plus what I'm doing is creating what I've got. I can't change the way the world is. All I can change is what I am doing in response to it.

If you are not satisfied with what you have, if you're say-ing, "I want something different but I don't know what it is," then there are four things to do. The first is to look at people you admire or those people that you're jealous of, and ask your-self, "What is it about their life or their lifestyle that I am jeal-ous of?" It might be that they're in the arts, they have more money, they're free, they're more creative, or they travel more.

Number two is to do a life purpose exercise, of which there are a number of versions running around in seminars and in books. If you discover your purpose is, let's say, to share love, well there are a lot of ways you can do that. You can do that as a parent. You can do that as a seminar leader for the *Course in Miracles*. You can do that as a massage therapist, etc.

Then you can take an aptitude testing. There's a current theory that says that there are seven forms of intelligence: spa-tial intelligence, emotional intelligence, kinesthetic intelligence, intellectual intelligence, etc. Knowing which you're strongest in can help lead you to a satisfying career.

The third thing you can do is simply what I call "try-ons." You say, "Okay I know I'm not happy doing this, let me try on something else." If you keep trying on things, you'll find some-thing that satisfies you more. It's called the "leaning into it" method. You lean into something to see how it feels. Maybe you want to be a public speaker, start giving some talks at schools. Maybe you want to travel more, start by taking a long vacation. Maybe you can be a travel agent. Maybe you can be a tour guide. You have to do something that excites you and that you have passion for. There are so many possibilities.

And the last thing you can do is to make a list of ten things you really love. When I first did that, I found out that I love to hang around smart people, I love to talk, I love to answer my mail, I love to read new things and learn new things. When you're done with your list, ask yourself, "What kind of profession would allow me to do that?" You could run a retreat center, run a publishing company, or have a think tank organization. There are a lot of professions that would allow you to do all the things on your list. Then you lean into them.

A lot of people think that the purpose of achieving goals is all the goodies you get along the way: nice car, nice house, getting to go on vacations, etc. And you do get those benefits if you choose to purchase those things. However, all of us know people who lost them. Donald Trump lost his for a while. I know an author who had everything he could possibly imagine and then his house burned down, including all his manuscripts; even his computer melted. But what the author didn't lose, and what Donald Trump didn't lose, and what you can't lose, is everything that you've become on the level of skills you've developed, knowledge bases that you've expanded, and the consciousness that you've achieved.

If you look at the transpersonal/spiritual teachings, most of them talk about expanding your capacity to love and expanding your wisdom. My point of view is that wisdom is that which relates to the practical, like when your wife asks you if she's fat, don't answer! The practical side of spirituality is how to apply wisdom in your everyday life so that you have more fulfillment for yourself and help create more fulfillment for others.

We are working on a program to get a *Chicken Soup for the Soul*® book in the hands of every prisoner in America. There are 1.3 million people in prisons and we've sent out about 50,000 books so far. We are now working with corporations to underwrite it at a much larger level. We also realized that we ought to write a book called *Chicken Soup for a Prisoner's Soul* that is directly aimed at them, written by prisoners for prisoners, so we've also done that.

And then at a global level, we're working on a book called *Chicken Soup for a Global Soul.* Each story would be from a different country—it would be 101 stories from 101 countries. Like all the *Chicken Soup for the Soul* books, it will cover issues like love, parenting, school, death and dying, dreams, overcoming obstacles, wisdom, etc. We're hoping that if a mother in Zaire is reading about a mother in Paris, and if a mother in Paris is reading about a mother in Zaire, that they both are going to think, "Wow! That mother is just like me." So perhaps it will lead to a little more empathic awareness that we all have the same needs, goals, wants, desires, fears, etc., as human beings. It doesn't matter what color we are, what religion we are, what nationality we are; we are really much more alike than we are different. That's really the essence of all the *Chicken Soup for the Soul*® books.

for reflection

Are you feeling "stuck" in your career? Are you working more, but enjoying it less? Then you need to begin the journey of rediscovering your soul's longings. As Jack says, changing what you're doing is tough. But it is really tougher to go through life not having taken the opportunity to live your dreams.

Are there other areas in your life that are not satisfying? Name them. Ask yourself what you need to change, let go of, or accept, in each area you name to be able to feel more satisfied. Then do as Jack says and make a list of the ten things you love to do. Start opening to the possibility that you can do what you love and make money, too.

To go after your dream takes chutzpah, courage, conviction, and trust that the spirit within you will help you navigate through any fear that arises. You're going to have to be honest with yourself and you will have to think deeply about what cause, action, or course in life would make you feel more alive and make life more worthwhile.

And don't be afraid to talk to a friend, a counselor, or someone who can reflect back to you your goals and dreams. Allow yourself to discover that thing or job or act that makes your heart flutter with nervousness and excitement. And through this process of discovery, you will be healed of every self-limiting, self-doubting belief you ever had. You will also be making a positive contribution to the world.

Creativity and prosperity

■ REV. EDWENE GAINES

Rev. Edwene Gaines is one of the most popular New Thought lecturers in the country. A frequent speaker at both Unity and Science of Mind Churches, Edwene's principles of prosperity combine prayer with practicality. Her new book, *The Four Spiritual Laws of Prosperity,* describes her principles. By practicing these principles, she believes that anyone can manifest her heart's desires. Edwene's own rags-to-riches life story attests to the truth of her teachings.

Edwene conveys the certainty of knowing she's a precious child of God. She knows her value and worth are unlimited. She believes that we're here to become bhodisattvas, or self-realized human beings. With down to earth honesty, Edwene shows us how.

We are so loved, and if we give this power, whatever it is—I call it God—a chance, it will respond to us; but we have to ask. I take time every day to first be grateful for all the good I have, then I ask for what I want, expecting to receive it. What stops people from doing that is fear. Most people stop themselves from acting on their creative ideas. I call them Divine ideas—those inspirations, the things that come to us that say "Oh wouldn't be fun to . . . Wouldn't it be fun to . . . I would if I could pay for it, if I had the money." Most people stop themselves from expressing their creativity because they are afraid. They use an excuse: I don't have the money. I don't have the time. I don't have the energy. I don't have the talent. All of this negative self-talk keeps us from acting on that inspiration of creativity that comes to us. Every one of us has access to millions of creative ideas and I believe that's what we are to do. We are to create. One of the terms that's used in this day and age is "co-creators with God." What we have the capacity to do has value whether it's fingerpainting, writing books, or performing on Broadway. There's all this creativity in us just waiting to express itself, but we put a lid on it because we have all these reasons why we can't express it. We get stuck. I think most of the illness we have can be found in people who are stuffing their creativity. If you're out there doing what you love to do, you don't have time to be sick. There is a loving presence which I happen to call God. You can call it mind or you can call it the energy that grows the trees. I have to come to the belief that there is something larger than us that did create and empower us, and loves us enough to look after us. With that belief system, anyone can move through fear. I'm not sure that fear ever goes away, but we can move through it and keep going in spite of the fear.

Fear is like a wall that keeps us stuck; in paralysis. I consider it just a signal for me to pay attention—to pay more attention to what I'm doing and really focus. I think that the purpose of fear is to warn us that we are going into something that we may have not done before.

The first step in creating anything is asking "Father, what must I change about myself to achieve what I want to achieve?" That really brings up fear because most of us, even though we might not be happy in what we're doing, are in a comfort zone. To step out of that comfort zone is going to require that we make some changes. It may mean that you're going to have to go out and ask for a raise, or start a business, or tell someone that a relationship is not working. You know the law is the cliché: you either grow or you die. And growth means change.

In being willing to grow, you are giving yourself permission to make mistakes. It's not that we necessarily learn by what we call mistakes. Even a child, when it's learning how to walk, plops down every once in a while in the process. We don't call that process a mistake, we call it practice. That's what we have to do. We have to practice the principles we believe in and sometimes it's going to feel like we've plopped down. Well that isn't a failure; it means we just have to practice some more. That's all it is, but you have to have that willingness. People who live in a comfort zone never have very exciting lives.

There's a quote that goes: "Courage is the commitment to begin without any guarantee of success." So you have to have courage and a belief in the possibility that there's something inside of you that's greater than the way you're functioning right now. In order to find that, you have to break those bars of behavior that have kept you in prison. You have to do some new things. Take some risks. Ask for greater wisdom. Ask for creative divine ideas to come to you, and then have the courage to step right up and say OK, that's mine; I'm going to act on it!

A lot of us, including me, became addicted to approval. Thank God I've broken most of my addiction to approval. I haven't broken all of it, but I give myself permission to do what I do and I give myself permission to accept that other people may not like it. I think that's part of the process of creativity: when you first start, if you're really being creative, you are doing something that's never been done before. The people around you may not understand what you're doing until you complete it. When you complete it, they will probably be your biggest supporters, but when you're first getting started, they may out of concern or fear for you, or just plain antagonistic behavior, criticize, condemn or complain about what you're doing. They're just doing their job, which is to criticize you. Your job is to accept it or not. I no longer choose to accept it. I choose to keep on going.

Quarreling never solved anything. I state my position and you state yours. If your position is different, well maybe I'll learn something, But I don't believe that my position versus your position over and over solves anything. It just wastes time. It's very good for people who are addicted to drama. I don't have time for drama. I have too many wonderful things to do.

In order to hold on to thoughts of anger, bitterness, revenge, guilt, and shame, we have to use a lot of energy. That's because we have to keep rehearsing stuff over and over to keep it alive. All that energy we use to keep rehearsing our grudges, shame, bitterness and thoughts of revenge could be used to create a new book, a new painting, a new piece of music, a new relationship, or a new bank account. If we can forgive and let go, we can use our energy in any way we want to. Every person on this planet has twenty-four hours every day. You can spend that time with thoughts of revenge or unforgiveness, or you can spend that time doing something that makes the world a better, more fun place to be.

for reflection

To be creative and live a fulfilling life, we must accept the idea that life is growth, and growth means change. Fear is the obstacle to growth. People who live in a state of fear imprison themselves. Their lives are static and unchanging and they worship the status quo. Change is seen as dangerous. They live terrified, bitter, frustrated lives.

Sit in a relaxed position. Think of something you want to change in your life. Change always generates fear. Take some time and look at all your fears in your mind's eye. You notice a large paper bag is on your lap. Grab your fears and stuff them in the bag and twist the opening shut. There is a fireplace in the wall. The flames are very high. Throw the paper bag full of your fears into the flames. See the flames burst the bag and burn up your fears. Think again of something you want to change in your life. What attitudes must you change if you are to get what you want?

Change comes from within. Any change you wish to see happen outside yourself must first be changed within yourself. Ask your intuition, God, the universe, or any power you believe in that is greater than yourself to help you change. Be still a moment and allow that power to work within you.

Then, open your eyes, get up and see how relaxed you feel. Get on with your life and allow the changemaking process to work within you.

Realizing one's dreams

■ JOHN PERKINS

John Perkins is the founder of Dream Change Coalition (www. dreamchange.org). The Dream Change Coalition seeks to change the prevailing western dream of greed and waste to one that is aligned with honoring the Earth and creating a sustainable future. John is intimately connected to successful ways of utilizing alternative energy resources. He was the president and CEO of a major U.S. alternative energy corporation.

The Dream Change Coalition is based on Perkins' work with indigenous cultures all over the world. Indigenous cultures know the power of dreams to create reality. A former Peace Corps volunteer, John has lived with indigenous peoples on every continent and has studied their healing traditions for the past thirty years. He has been a consultant to the United Nations, World Bank, and many Fortune 500 companies. John's books include *Shapeshifting, The World Is As You Dream It,* and *Spirit of the Shuar,* which shares the wisdom of the Amazon tribe that still lives and works the way it has for hundreds of years. John teaches the shamanistic practices of the Shuar and other indigenous peoples in the workshops he conducts worldwide. The purpose of the workshops is to help people realize their dreams. John's vision of creating a positive future prompted the writing of his latest book, *Confessions of an Economic Hit Man.*

In this essay, John talks about manifesting our own dreams at the same time we are manifesting a collective dream for peace on earth.

When you look around, you know that this world of human societies was created by sleeping people, because awake, aware, conscious people would create a very different world. None of the quick fixes to the world's problems are going to work, unless we change the dream of greed and scarcity that the world is dreaming. The United States is selling this dream to the rest of the world. We are extremely good at seducing other countries into buying the dream. Our message of wanting "more, better, bigger, and faster" is even seductive to us. For example, I live a much more material life than I want to, or should, because it's so damn easy. But if I didn't have a material life that made me look successful, then I would lose my credibility. If I want to host a dinner at my house to promote conservation or saving the rainforest, then I had better have a nice house that people will want to come to.

While I lived with indigenous tribes, we did a lot of dreaming about things that are truly spiritual. We dreamt about having good food and clean water; we dreamt about having love; we dreamt about wanting our children to inherit these things. All of the indigenous people I've worked with around the world dream about the same things. They don't worry about what they're going to have for breakfast tomorrow morning; they know that either breakfast will be there or it won't be, and they don't have to make a lot of decisions about it. The bananas are going to be ripe, or the papayas are going to be ripe, or whatever is going to be ripe.

When the U.S. has gone into indigenous cultures, they bring a dream that revolves around possessions. The U.S.

dream says that there's something substandard about you unless you have the right clothes, car, or house. But people have to realize that's a dream manufacturers try to sell you. Manufacturers have become the authorities of what you dream. As kids we learned to relinquish our power to those people who were authorities, i.e., the teacher or the principal. As we listen to the Posts, Kelloggs, General Mills, General Motors, General Electrics, and all the Generals out there, we are accepting them as authorities. They hire authorities to further convince us of their authority. They hire an actor who has the voice of Darth Vader telling you that you need their products. You're told, with great authority, that if you don't use the right toothpaste nobody is going to love you. You also get people like Britney Spears selling Pepsi Cola. This is the dream that is being marketed to indigenous people all over the world. It's a dream that we've all bought into.

In indigenous cultures, the role of the shaman is to wake people up and also to inspire them to direct their energies in ways that will shapeshift their world. The shaman helps people learn what their dreams are and then helps them realize their dreams. In our culture, we tell people what their dreams should be. That's what television is all about, that's what advertising is about, that's what the authority figures are constantly doing.

There are several elements in the shape shifting process. The first is that you need to know what your dream and your mission are. The second element is that you have to be committed to your dream. The third is that you have to apply energy to make that dream come true.

How much energy, time, and patience you need for a dream to manifest depends on what your dream is. If you have a big dream that revolves around changing the world, it is going to take a tremendous amount of energy, time, patience, and courage. But, at the same time, if you're committed to manifesting a big dream, it's important to have a lot of little dreams. We need to have our dreams come true from time to time in order to keep ourselves going. One of my dreams is to change the world. But I have to have a lot of little dreams, too, like having a book published. These little dreams will feed the larger dreams, like stepping stones on the journey.

All we need to do to create any change we want is to apply energy, whether it's finding a cure for cancer, saving a forest, or building a house. What keeps us from applying that energy is our fears. So we have to identify those fears. In the workshops, we teach that people's lives are like the journeys that are written about in the great epic poems like *Beowulf, The Odyssey, The Iliad,* or even *Star Wars.*

Joseph Campbell has talked about how we are all on a hero's journey. In one of his books he said that we have to create new myths. I was with the Dalai Lama and a group of twenty-nine Dream Change Coalition people several years ago. One of the people asked him what it would take for there to be world peace. The Dalai Lama, without even giving it a second thought, said, "Responsibility and compassion."

We will never have peace for all of humanity until we also dream a dream of peace for every sentient creature on earth including insects and animals. World peace will not occur while we are letting human populations grow uncontrollably at the same time that our use of natural resources continues to grow uncontrollably. Peace for future generations of all creatures that inhabit the earth will not happen unless we make sure that we are not wasting resources and encroaching on animal and plant habitats. In South Florida, we're using up our resources far too fast and we're destroying plants and animals. Today, we need to drastically change the way we interact with each other and our environment. If we are to survive we must rise to new levels of consciousness. A good place to start is to dream a dream of responsibility and compassion towards all sentient creatures on earth. Then you must commit to making that dream come true by taking the actions you need to take to support it.

for reflection

John Perkins believes that in order to be awakened we must learn to dream. Your dream is your mission and purpose in life. In order to realize your dream, you need to know three things. First, what is your purpose? Second, are you committed to your purpose? Third, are you willing to apply constant energy to make this dream come true? Sit comfortably, and close your eyes. Take a few deep breaths and relax, relax, relax. Now, think of something that is terribly important to you personally. For some, the most important thing personally is to follow their bliss. Whatever comes to mind, focus on it. Hold it as a vision in your mind. See it in Technicolor. Allow it to expand, to fill the walls of your mind. Listen to the words and music that spring forth from this vision. Enjoy this multimedia display. Know that you are committed to making this dream a reality. It is important to follow a single vision and not be swayed or seduced by other ideas. If any other ideas intrude, see them written on a piece of paper. Fold the paper they are written on in half, and now you have a paper airplane. Throw the plane out into the darkness. See it disappear into the void. This takes discipline, and you are capable of the focusing necessary to accomplish this. Promise yourself that you will commit some time each day to energize this dream; it may be ten minutes or an hour depending on circumstances. Start planning each step to realize your dream, or to be precise, your self-realization. Count backwards from ten to one. When you reach one your eyes will snap open and you will immediately apply the daily dose of energy that will make this dream an awakened reality.

spiritual
relationships
& sexuality

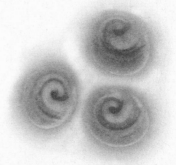

Creating sacred relationships

■ DIANE CIRINCIONE, PH.D.
AND GERALD G. JAMPOLSKY, M.D.

Jerry Jampolsky and Diane Cirincione are teachers of peace. Their many books and tapes all carry the message that forgiveness is the most important healing tool that anyone can ever cultivate. A child psychiatrist by training, Jerry started the Center for Attitudinal Healing in 1975. His landmark book, *Love Is Letting Go of Fear*, started many spiritual seekers on their path. Diane is a clinical psychologist, an author, and an international lecturer. Jerry and Diane have lectured and consulted on "Practical Spirituality" in over fifty countries, working with individuals, organizations, governments, and businesses. They are the recipients of many awards given for their humanitarian work.

Among the books that Diane and Jerry have co-authored are: *Change Your Mind, Change Your Life; Love Is the Answer: Creating Positive Relationships;* and *Wake-Up Calls*. Diane is the sole author of *Sounds of the Morning Sun*.

Jerry and Diane have been together for more than twenty years and married for more than ten. In their workshops and lectures about healing relationships, they openly share stories about their own relationship healing. This makes their teaching real, warm, and very human. They share below several tools and techniques that have helped their relationship thrive.

Jerry: Diane and I define the word intimacy by separating the word out phonetically, "in-to-me-see." "In-to-me-see" is the thing we want the most and the thing we fear the most. It takes a lot of courage to be intimate; to go as deep as you're willing to go.

We do our best to have no secrets with each other in our relationship. We know that secrets get in the way of intimacy. We have the willingness to share everything including our dreams. One of the twelve principles of Attitudinal Healing is seeing other people as either extending love or being fearful. It's easy to see someone who is acting out on the street as calling for love. But when it's a person you live with or a person you're close to who is acting out, it's harder to see that person as calling for love. You think they are attacking you or trying to manipulate you.

When Diane and I wake up in the morning (at 4:30), the first thing we do is say a prayer reminding ourselves that peace of mind is our only goal for that day. The prayer comes from *A Course in Miracles*:

I am not a body I am free for I am still as God created me.

I want the peace of God.

The peace of God is everything I want.

The peace of God is my one goal; the aim of all my living here, the end I seek, my purpose, and my function and my life, while I abide where I am not at home.

That prayer has been like a rudder of a ship. But so many relationships come together because of neediness. The other person is filling a hole in your heart. The relationship is based on how much you can get, not what you can give. It doesn't mean that people shouldn't come together for those reasons, because I think we are drawn together for our differences as well as our similarities. It's just a question of, when we do come together, what do we do then? Do we just continue to work to fulfill our neurotic needs, or can we really begin to look more deeply at why we're together?

Diane: A lot of people say they don't even know if they're well matched at all. In reality, they are probably perfectly matched because they're working out what they need to work out, just like Jerry and I are, and everybody else is. We tend to leave our relationships thinking we're going to find just the opposite in another relationship. Often we find that what looks like the opposite on the surface is the same challenge underneath. That's not saying we should or shouldn't leave relationships; it means that if we're leaving because of something we're not going to deal with in this relationship, more than likely, we are going to find it in the next one. The more conscious we are about our processes, the better the choices we can make for ourselves.

Part of intimacy is learning to have a harmonious relationship with yourself. If you're condemning yourself, even if you think it is justified, it's important to ask whether this justified condemnation is really bringing you peace of mind. We do that in our relationship. We ask ourselves whether self-condemnation is really bringing us the peace of God. And the answer, of course, is no. We see that there's no value in carrying on the anger and we see more value in transforming that anger into love.

Another view is that our egos (or our personalities) want to dump all over ourselves. One thing that's been helpful for us is to realize that we have certain patterns in our lives, and the patterns themselves are not necessarily what will change. But the way we deal with the patterns will change, and then the way we create our lives will change. So instead of being as harsh on ourselves as we used to be, we now look at ourselves and laugh. We'll say, "Well look at that. Look at what you did, you're an interesting person." It's really helped us be kinder to ourselves.

Jerry: One of the things that we have found helpful in our relationship is that we each take responsibility for our own experience of what is happening. If we're upset, either Diane or I will come to the other with these simple words, "I need help." That signifies that there is something the troubled one wants to share, and is willing to take responsibility that it's not the other person's fault. It means that either Diane or I need to be listened to. It is a very important process. It's changed a lot of relationships and saved a lot of marriages.

What prevents people from experiencing peace in relationships is having a script for a situation. If the expectations attached to that script are not met, then they will lose their peace. Let's be practical about it. When we first began our relationship, I had a script saying that when you were at a party and you were about ready to leave and you were saying your good-byes, you were going to leave in three or four minutes. Diane—she's Italian—had a script saying that getting ready to leave a party and saying goodbyes was just the beginning of a ceremony, and twenty-five minutes later, she was still leaving. It was very upsetting to me that she wasn't keeping what I thought of as her agreement. But she was seeing it differently, because to her saying good-bye was a process, so she didn't see any disagreement at all. We really dug and came up with new scripts for each other. I said that Diane's way of saying good-bye was Italian and my way of saying good-bye was Jewish. Most of the time I'm okay with Italian good-byes, but there are times when I might be "peopled out" and I say, "Diane, I really need your help tonight. I really need a Jewish good-bye." Then we're out the door. The idea is that we never take for granted what a situation is going to be like. We have a way of communicating that gives each of us an opportunity to have a voice in what our needs are at the moment; then between us, we decide what we're going to do in a quick shorthand way.

Diane: Another thing we learned in our relationship is that pleasing someone doesn't necessarily mean loving someone. Loving someone is giving that person your truest honesty, which means your integrity and your harmony in what you're thinking, saying, and doing. We recognize that the other person's guidance is their guidance and that our lives are committed to supporting the other person's guidance. That practice has always been nourishing to the relationship.

Diane and Jerry: For us, again, it comes down to asking our guidance how we need to be in that moment and what we need to think, to say, or do. In our particular relationship, we never taking anything for granted. We don't even take for granted who's going to drive the car or who's going to take out the garbage. When you let go of your expectations, every day is new. It's a wonderful way of keeping everything fresh in the relationship.

for reflection

An intimate relationship is a voyage of exploration. In order to undertake this voyage, we must let go of all expectations. Most expectations are romantic ones. We expect our partners to think and behave in certain ways. Then "he doesn't bring me flowers anymore" signals the end of a relationship. If we cannot let our expectations go, we will never see the other person as they really are. We will only see them as a mask that we have invented in our own imagination.

Trust is very important. It runs two ways. If we cannot trust ourselves to be open and honest, how can we trust anyone else?

Humility, the idea that "I might need help," creates openness and honesty. You are asking for input in the decision-making process.

Being able to say "no" as well as "yes" keeps us from sacrificing unnecessarily and feeling put upon.

These ideas are guidelines to creating an intimate relationship, one of absolute honesty, integrity, and unconditional love.

Spirituality, intimacy, and creating real relationships

■ ARMAND DIMELE

Armand DiMele is the founder of the DiMele Center, a treatment and learning facility with a holistic approach in New York City. Armand is also the renowned host of the "Positive Mind" radio show that airs on WBAI in New York City. He is the co-author of *Repairing Your Marriage after His Affair: A Guide for Healing and Rebuilding Trust* with Marcella Weiner.

Armand's hallmark is helping people fuse feelings and knowledge through a true compassion. Armand believes that when people really understand themselves, the world will be more loving, and, in turn, there will be less violence and hatred in the world.

Whether he's speaking to one person in a private therapy session or speaking to thousands of people on the radio, Armand provides a space of complete safety. He's the quintessential "everything-is-going-to-be-okay" therapist and best friend rolled into one.

The key to all good relationships is that somewhere inside of them, each person has enough sense of self that they can accept somebody as their partner who is not totally dependent, and is somebody who chooses to be in the relationship. This means that each partner has a good relationship with himself or herself. The old standard for a relationship was that it was comfortable to have somebody around, or it felt good to have a warm body around. But to have a spiritual relationship, you have to have two fully integrated human beings making a connection. That's not easy. It seems easier to slide into the comfort of having a warm body around to watch TV or eat a meal with. But those kinds of relationships don't allow you to connect with your authentic self. Spiritual relationships have a new form. The new form of relationship has two people who are really connected with themselves, which means that they are honest. Honesty means that they face each other and tell the truth about what they are thinking or feeling without fear of losing the other. You have to take the risk of losing the person by being honest. When you do that, you are going to have a much higher level of relationship.

In order to tell that truth, you have to know what the truth is. That means you can't be hiding from yourself. You have to be honest with yourself, knowing what you feel at the moment. When you know that, then you have a true connection with yourself. A person who is living in accord with her real self does not have the need to get other people to love her.

To have a real relationship with somebody, you cannot spend your time trying to keep him or her from leaving. The other day, a woman told me she realized that when she told her boyfriend who she was, he was going to leave her. They were always going out to noisy bars where he would meet his friends. She told him that she didn't like going out to noisy places, and she really needed quiet time. The reason she didn't tell him sooner was that she knew he would think she was boring, which he did. He decided to leave her. She said, "I'm probably going to have to cry every day for the next year to get over this." I thought that was such a profound thing, because what she was saying was, "There will be a loss and I'll suffer the pain, but I'll move on." Being able to feel pain is an essential part of being an adult. Children avoid pain. A true adult says that something may hurt, but I'll do it anyway.

To have a spiritual relationship, you have to love yourself. Self-love means you look at yourself with all your warts and say, "You're really okay, kiddo." Self-love is being able to smile at the kid in the mirror. Self love means you value yourself and think you are worthy. When you decide to be real, then you are making the journey to your core, spiritual nature. This is the essence of self-acceptance. When you accept yourself, other people will come along who will respect you and who will be attracted to you.

Every date should be a *ménage à quatre*: I and my relationship with myself go out with you and your relationship with yourself. There are four entities: I have a relationship with myself and you have a relationship with yourself, and the four of us go out together.

People get involved in a dysfunctional relationship because they have needs, which they go about satisfying in funny ways. Sometimes they go for sex; sometimes they go for security. There's really nothing wrong or bad in dysfunctional relationships. There's an Israeli joke: a man marries a woman and for the next twenty years he wants to keep her the way she is; the woman marries the man and she spends the next twenty years trying to change him. But a relationship that's based on trying to change the other will never be satisfying.

I believe that people who get to know themselves won't create wars; people won't have a need to kill people. When people get to know and understand themselves, they will be more loving. There won't be a need to perpetuate violence and hatred. When people go within and connect with themselves, they realize they are connected to the universe and they are connected to all living things.

for reflection

Armand DiMele talks about real relationships as opposed to superficial relationships. He feels that only people willing to be open and completely honest have chance of having a real or very intimate relationship.

Let's explore our own thoughts. Think of relationships that you've gone through. At the start of a relationship, have you been in the habit of "putting your best foot forward," creating an image of yourself that is shiny and glamorous and untouched by wounds or scars? Have you hid your "socially unacceptable" parts of yourself from your partner? The psychologist Sigmund Freud discovered that repressed feelings and thoughts won't stay down in the pressure cooker of the unconscious mind for long. These ignored thoughts or feelings are projected out unconsciously in inappropriate ways. Have you ever said to yourself, "Why did I say that, why did I do that?"

Only mature, self-accepting people can have or real or spiritual relationships with each other. Would you be willing, when you start a new relationship, to be open and honest and free with all your feelings and thoughts?

You are enough as you are

■ HANS CHRISTIAN KING

Hans Christian King is a psychic medium. Through his gifts of clair-voyance and clairaudience, he is able to see and hear spirits. Through his gift of clairsentience, he is able to feel their feelings and person-alities. Thousands and thousands of people have been helped by messages that Hans transmits from loved ones in the spirit world. The highly specific messages he receives from the spirit world assure the loved ones remaining on this side of the continuity of life after death. In his group workshops, even people who do not receive personal messages from the other side gain the knowledge that love is the reality that binds our level of existence to that of the hereafter.

Hans is also a spiritual teacher. His teachings offer insight and wisdom into how to create a happier, more meaningful life while we are on the earth plane. The key to finding happiness, according to Hans, is recognizing one's own goodness and self-worth. Guilt and shame are human-made constructs; God loves us just as we are.

O ur society has a tendency to make sex an issue. There is no issue. Sex just is. There is no right or wrong. There is no straight. There is no gay. There's just sexuality and sexuali-ty is spirituality. Gender identity is something you choose before you come onto this plane. I become sad when I see so many gay people suffering because society has taught them that they are something less than perfect. There is so much guilt associated with sex. What we have done to our children is so horrific that it boggles the mind! We teach our children that the natural act of sexual intimacy is wrong. This is unbelievable; sexuality is really a gift. On top of that, if someone gets a sexually transmitted disease, they then believe that somehow they deserved it. They believe God is punishing them.

I believe in a God of Love and a God of Love doesn't punish anybody. We have disenfranchised our own children because of a religious belief. I used to work with the naval services and counseled suicidal young men. Almost every young man I spoke to needed a hug from a man, but thought that was homosexuality. In this country, we have to teach our children that they are enough. I've been saying that for forty years. Who they are is enough. There's nothing they need to do or become. They are in themselves perfect examples of the love of God.

If someone came to me who had contracted HIV or hepatitis through a sexual act I would say, "What wonder can we find in this for you? What can you learn from this? What is your soul going to be able to get out of this?" Feeling guilty inhibits the body and inhibits healing. There's a part of the mind that thinks, "I deserved this."

Younger generations are more comfortable with their gender identity. They are not nearly as inhibited. One of the good things about MTV and VH1 is that they incorporate sexuality into the music and into the shows. The TV show *Will and Grace* has brought homosexuality into the living rooms of mainstream America. In my day, movies portrayed the gay lifestyle as tragic. Gay love is no different than straight love. But gay people have been taught that there is something wrong with them. When people think there is something wrong with them, they search for love in order to fill emotional and physical neediness. Making love when one is in a state of self-actualization is different than having sex out of physical or emotional neediness. Making love in a state of self-actualization is bliss; it's Divine. Sex is the essence of Spirit in manifestation. Sex is the energy of life. It's natural to feel sexual.

As I said before, you chose your sexuality prior to being born in this lifetime, based on what you need to learn. The main lesson you need to learn is "I AM. I am enough!" The most important technique you can practice, to make yourself realize that you are enough, is to not listen to the mind chatter that's present in your conscious mind. That's where the programming is. Every time you have a thought that you're a bad boy or a bad girl, you have to turn to it and say, "No, that's not true." You have to say to yourself, "I'm enough. I am perfect. I am God's child. Nothing can harm me." It sounds so simple, but if you do that, you will reprogram your consciousness. You will claim the love and light that are your birthright.

for reflection

Hans Christian King notes that you are enough. You are as God created you and He does not make mistakes. Many people in today's society do not feel they are good, whole, or even enough. These negative ideas of social conditioning are harmful to our well-being. Sit quietly for a moment. Close your eyes. See yourself in your mind's eye, enveloped in a golden light. This is the light of spirit. Say to yourself three times:

I am enough just the way I am.

I am a Holy Child of God. God does not make mistakes.

I am perfect just the way God made me.

Repeat this exercise every day for one week. You will find that after a week's time your self image will start to shift and change. If you ever feel fearful, afraid, unwanted, or guilty, repeat these exercises for another week.

Relationships as a spiritual practice

■ STEPHEN AND ONDREA LEVINE

Stephen and Ondrea Levine are exceptional teachers of life and living. Both have been involved in the field of conscious dying for more than thirty years. In addition, they coauthored the book *Embracing the Beloved: Relationships As a Path of Awakening* and have presented numerous workshops and lectures about relationship. Stephen's latest book, *Unattended Sorrow*, continues the work of deep healing found in his earlier books *Who Dies* and *Healing into Life and Death*, as well as in his many others.

Together Stephen and Ondrea share the wisdom gained in over twenty years of "being" with one another through both the heights and depths of intimate relationship. They believe that true intimacy lies in developing compassion for another's pain. The gift they bring to anyone who has ever tried to follow the path of relationship, or to anyone who would like to try relationship as a spiritual path, is the voice of absolute authenticity about the process. They realize that to love and accept another human being is truly to love and accept one's self. They offer a grounded spirituality based on being completely aware of the frailties and glories of being human.

In the process of fearlessly exploring their own humanity, they provide an infinitely compassionate space to which others can come for healing.

Relationships can be described as a Yoga, or a spiritual practice that leads to union. Every spiritual practice has certain elements that people perform. The basic spiritual practice of relationships is honesty. It takes tremendous courage to be honest. In the course of your relationship with someone, if honesty is the basis, then you are cultivating other qualities such as courage,straightforwardness, patience, and non-guarding. You're uncluttering your mind. You're opening your heart. And what Ondrea and I have found is that it's easier said than done. We still ask, "How many levels of letting go do I have to go through before what comes out of my mouth is what's in my heart completely?"

A second element of relationship practice is letting go: the letting go of that which blocks our connectedness. It is just loving the other person as she is. And that takes a lot because we don't love ourselves as is. This process of loving someone else is really the process of coming to love ourselves.

One of the wonderful things about being with a loved one when he or she dies is that a lot of stuff that blocks love comes up. It's not just a wonderful loving, healing—supernatural healing—for the heart; it also defines the places where the heart has a difficult time being present.

There are no enlightened people; there are only enlightened actions. There are no self-hating people; there are only self-hating actions. The person inside is vast space, a boundaryless luminescence. What floats in it, we mistake for who we really are. In Western psychology they say that if you have something in potential, that's who you are. If they really realized what we really have as potential is everything from God to the devil, then they would stop saying that.

It's in there; it's all in everyone. Mother Theresa gets the Noble Prize and what's the first thing out of her mouth, "Oh, I'm not worthy." We laugh and say it's funny, but what came out of her mouth is pure rank ego. To say I'm no good is just the same as saying I am good. It's just talking about yourself— just defining yourself. It's just forgetting you are God. To say I'm wonderful or terrible are both just as ignorant. I'm remarkable! That's the truth! And sometimes I'm remarkably stupid. And sometimes I'm remarkably lovely.

The difficulty in opening up to another is the difficulty in opening up to your own heart. There is no difference between somebody else's confusion and your confusion. When you get into it being mine or yours, you get into heaven and hell and you miss paradise. Paradise is now.

In Buddhist psychology, they say (Robert Thurman was the first to put it out) that the clearest time for you to see the self is when you've been insulted. You see that righteous innocence arise in something that knows itself much better than that. When you hear that righteousness arise, you know you're starting to approach some of that soft quicksand of the ego. True innocence is exactly the opposite. But that righteous innocence, of, "I didn't do anything!"—we've done everything! What haven't we done? True innocence is being nobody. Righteousness is I'm a God. I'm a saint, or I'm a good person.

Relationships identify what obstructs or closes our hearts and work from there. Relationship is such a difficult practice.

You know relationship and death are similar: it brings out the best and the worst in most people.

The relationship you have with your partner, when it's the right relationship, is the same relationship you have with God: pure surrender. Without trust you can't do it. You have to have trust between two people before you can have that kind of openness; that kind of honesty. There's a reason for that, too. This isn't just spiritual interest. This is learned, worldly, self-respect. Relationships bring out the best in you and the worst in you. People hurt you. People who ordinarily wouldn't lie in the outside world, lie incredibly in a relationship. It's not really lying, but they are dishonest emotionally and maybe even intellectually. This is because relationships bring out the most fear in them. People *do* say I love you and don't mean it. People *do* say let's have a mutual bank account and then they empty that bank account. It doesn't happen that often, but we hear about it often enough to cause us to distrust. Something like that only has to happen to a person once or twice for her to have a generic distrust of others. It would only take having an alcoholic parent or a forgetful teacher who used his hands in the wrong way to develop that level of mistrust.

Trust can also mean that it's okay for you to have your space. You don't have to share; that's real trust. It's like if you had a wolf that you'd taken out of the wilderness and you wanted to make friends with it. The wolf is scared and when it's scared it will attack. It is attacking because it is afraid it will be attacked. Now if you try to smooch up that wolf, you would never get near it. But, if you were to go sit in the farthest corner of its cave and read a book, the wolf will eventually come up and lay in your lap. Don't threaten its space, just show that you are someone who can be trusted who's not there for her own pleasure at someone else's expense.

I don't know that people can let it all go, anyhow. I think you're in a relationship two years before you even know that you're in a relationship. That's why most people break off relationships at around two years-because they are starting to find out who they are and who the other person is and it's frightening. When you're relating to a person, you have to realize that you may be relating to their love, but you're also relating to all the fear they have and all their grief. People go into a relationship because they both like archeology, Miles Davis, or the color blue. But they also need to learn to relate on the level where both of them may have been hurt as children. Or perhaps they both had been dishonest with others and feel guilty about it. Each person is doing his or her own purification process. When they are in relationship together, it's really great if each one knows that they don't have to do the other's purification process. When, for example, I say, "I want to go mountain climbing," and you say, "I don't want to go mountain climbing," I'm the one who has to go mountain climbing, not you.

There are more opportunities for relationships than there ever were. As many men have read our relationship book as women. When we started our workshops, it was 95 percent women, then 85 percent, then 75 percent. Now it's almost even some places. So I think the men are becoming more conscious and the women are becoming sensitive to the way men are conscious or not conscious. I think it's come to the point that people don't want relationship unless it is conscious. They just don't want to do the other thing anymore. They may go out and have sex a couple of times a year because they want that relationship with their own body, but they don't want to be with another person unless it's going to be a whole-hearted relationship when you get to that place, nothing else will do.

for reflection

Steve and Ondrea Levine talk about relationships. But they are not talking about any relationship. They are talking about "wholehearted relationships."

In order to have a wholehearted relationship you must open your own heart, and that takes courage because opening yourself without censorship makes you vulnerable. Your defenses are gone, your heart is transparent, and all your pimples and warts are visible to the naked eye. You have to accept yourself and your partner as both loving, open and trusting, yet knowing that each one of you have issues that are not resolved, and may never be resolved. Showing compassion for each other's pain is one of the greatest gifts of love.

In romantic love the heart resonates to the splendid parts of the loved one and we magnify these lovely parts to encompass the whole person . . . and delude ourselves that we know the wholeness of this person. But underneath it all are the wounds and scars of past trials and tribulations. The psychologist Jung called this our dark side. The dark side will slide out of its hiding place of repression and will emerge in an unpleasant manner sooner or later.

Love is not enough to maintain a wholehearted relationship. Compassion, empathy, and acceptance are needed as well. The compassionate heart creates relationships here on earth that reflect heaven's purpose.

spiritual
awareness

Be the message

WALLY "FAMOUS" AMOS

Wally "Famous" Amos's mission in life is to be a messenger of inspiration. And by his presence, he does just that. He was born in Tallahassee, Florida, to a very strict mother who cultivated in him a strong sense of responsibility at an early age. But it was his Aunt Della who welcomed him into her home when he was twelve and showered him with unconditional love in the form of fabulous chocolate chip cookies. It was this cookie inspiration that helped launch the Famous Amos cookie company. Famous Amos cookies and the photo of Wally in a Panama hat and West Indian shirt became icons across the country. Despite serious setbacks, losing the Famous Amos company, experiencing lawsuits, and ups and downs with various other business ventures, Wally never stopped being a beacon for positive thinking. His inspirational story as well as his words of wisdom can be found in his many books including *The Cookie Never Crumbles: Practical Recipes for Everyday Living* and *Watermelon Magic: Seeds of Wisdom and Slices of Life.*

Wally has never stopped giving back to the community. He is a member of the Board of Directors of Communities in Schools and the National Center for Family Literacy.

Wally travels tirelessly across the country lecturing to diverse groups, from college students to business leaders, on the importance of holding true to vision. His flashing eyes, smiling face, and easy attitude communicate warmth, love, and acceptance. For Wally, inspiring others is what spiritual living is all about.

People's lives today are defined by how much money they make, what kind of house they live in, or how much stuff they have. But more and more I think people are discovering that accumulating things doesn't make them happy. I'm meeting a lot of people who are seeking spirituality and alternative means for happiness. They are seeking joy, instead of happiness. Happiness leads one towards materialism, because everything is so dependent on the exterior. If your exterior life is in order, then you are happy. But joy is from within. You can be joyful regardless of what is going on outside. That's where I want to live. I want to be joyful. I have no control of what's happening outside my life, but I have lots of control over what happens on the inside.

It takes surrender and trust to be joyful. It's trusting that the universe is in order. It's trusting that whatever you need will be provided. It's also surrendering to God's plans. For God does have a plan for us, even when it appears as if things are falling apart. I believe that every experience you have is a part of the universal plan; there's a path that you are meant to take. I learned so much from the experience of losing Famous Amos. It helped me to develop the belief system I have today. I just have to accept where I am, and the path that I have traveled; by doing so I become joyous to be alive. I have everything I need this second. What else is there?

It doesn't mean that I don't make plans. But sometimes when you make plans, God laughs. You plan but sometimes you might not realize that this plan or that plan might not be carried forth in your life. There are also people who don't plan.

They just wake up and say, "What is the universe going to offer me today?" And they live the life they choose to live. There is some degree of planning in my life, but I leave room for serendipity because that's where the adventure is. Not knowing, for me, is part of the adventure.

I've never had an excessive amount of money, although people think that I have. Much of my life has been meeting credit deadlines, but I always meet them and that's all you need to do. And the idea, for me, is to know that whatever my needs are, they will be fulfilled. I may not get what I want, but I always get what I need. Here's the thing: how much air do you need to breathe? You always have enough. You always get exactly what you need to sustain each breath. How much sunshine do you need? You always get enough of the things that really sustain you and absolutely matter in life. Why wouldn't you get enough material things? Material things are nothing without breathing. Someone once asked me what I liked best about life and I said breathing. I don't care how much money I've got; it has no meaning.

There are no excuses for failing to live your vision. You are only a victim of your own stupidity or your own arrogance or your own ego or the limitations you put on yourself. It is not the color of your skin that prevents you from being successful or from doing stuff. I am Black. I've been Black my whole life and I will be Black the rest of my life. When I wake up in the morning I look in the mirror and say, "You're still Black." Everyone can see I'm Black. So what! I never looked for any excuse to be a victim. It is the belief that you cannot do something because of the color of your skin. There are no limitations in being female. It's the belief. You buy into the societal belief that "I'm female," so you feel limited. Of course there are people who will try to limit you. There are people who will create barriers in your life. So what. Find a way around them, over them or through them. Believing you are limited will not bring you success.

I recently heard a speaker, Lance Secretan, who said that leaders have to inspire and not motivate. Motivation can be coercion. Inspiration is God-based. To inspire someone you have to get inside of them. You literally move them to action. I used to call myself an inspirational motivational speaker. But in listening to this talk I realized that I want to be a messenger of inspiration. I want to elevate the level of self-esteem in society. If I inspire you enough, then you'll do it yourself.

I've also never stopped giving back. Even when I was going through downturns in my business life, I still served nonprofit organizations because it's important to give. Sure, there are times when I don't have the money to cover all my expenses, but I think those are the times when I still need to give. I'm not interested in what you could do for me. It's fine receiving now and then. But, more than likely, I'll ask what I can do for you.

I'm not interested in impressing anyone. If I want to impress you, I will impress you with positive behavior, not with material stuff. I will impress you with what I am inside not with what I've got.

for reflection

Wally makes a distinction between the words happiness and joy. Happiness is fleeting; it comes and goes depending on external circumstances. Joy is everlasting. It resides deep down inside of us and cannot be extinguished by bad fortune. Is your life joyful? Have you known joy? What would have to change for you to experience more joy?

Spirit is all-loving and, as Wally says, has plans for your life. Do you believe Spirit can give you everything you need in life? What do you want that you don't need? What do you need but don't think will be provided for you?

Do you agree that people limit themselves by playing the victim? Do you have a victim consciousness? Do you limit yourself from achieving your dreams? What can you do to find a way around people who limit you?

Giving can often be a hard thing to do, especially when you feel you don't have anything to give. But we all have something to give. We may not have $1,000,000 to donate. We may not have the resources to build someone a house, or buy them new clothes, or give them food. But we do have our smiles, and our kind words, and our warm, loving embraces. What can you give? Who would you give to? Do you even want to give?

Enlighten up: laughter as a spiritual path

■ STEVE BHAERMAN

Steve Bhaerman is an author, comedian, and workshop leader, who has performed comedy for the past eighteen years as Swami Beyondananda. As the Swami, he has authored four books, including his latest, *Swami for Precedent: A 7-Step Plan to Heal the Body Politic and Cure Electile Dysfunction*. He has also produced such comedy audio tapes as *Yogi From Muskogee, Enlightening Strikes Again, Don't Squeeze the Shaman, Beyondananda and Beyond, The Fool's Journey, Drive Your Karma, Curb Your Dogma* and most recently *Supreme Court Jester*. He is also a noted "cosmic comedy coach" who works with authors, speakers, performers, healers, therapists, businesspeople, and educators to use comedy as a "healing art."

Steve is not only funny, he's smart. He was a political science major in college and his political savvy comes through in his comedy; so does his deep spirituality. Much of Steve's humor is based on wordplay. He tells people that to have peace in the world we have to become nomads, as in "I no mad at you" and "you no mad at me." Steve educates his audiences in addition to entertaining and enlightening them. He reminds us all not to take ourselves too seriously and he shows us how to do it.

Laughter heals. We've heard it so often, it's almost a cliché. There is the classic story of Norman Cousins, who treated a life-threatening illness by checking into a hotel room with Marx Brothers movies and Candid Camera reruns. When he

got well, the Medical Establishment decided to study the healing power of laughter—the logic being, "Well, it works in
practice, but does it work in theory?"

And indeed researchers found that laughter has proven
physiological benefits. Laughter produces endorphins, our
body's natural painkiller. Laughter improves immune function.
Hearty laughter is literally good for the heart, because when we
laugh it causes our blood vessels to dilate. And that is certainly
better than having them die early!

But laughter is medicine in the Native American sense as
well; a transformational tool that, used wisely, can bring not just
physical healing, but emotional release, mental flexibility, and
spiritual perspective. At its best, a joke or humorous moment
hits on "all four cylinders"—there is the physical and emotional
release during "ejoculation," there is the insight that follows in
the wake of the laughter, and there is the spiritual perspective
that comes from levity helping us "rise above" the situation and
see it from a higher perspective.

My favorite true story of the transformational power of
humor: At the time of the Cuban missile crisis, American and
Soviet delegates were meeting to discuss possible trade between
the two countries. When news of the missile crisis hit, everything stopped and there was tremendous tension in the room.
Finally, one of the Soviet delegates suggested that they go
around the room and each tell a joke. He volunteered to start:
"What is the difference between capitalism and communism?"

The answer: "In capitalism, man exploits man. In communism, it's the other way around." In the outburst of laugh-

ter came not just the release of tension, but the awareness that what we have in common as human beings transcends any of our man-made structures.

We can experience "enlightenment" any time we lighten up through levity, particularly when we choose to laugh at those things we consider the most serious. In his book *Man's Search for Meaning*, Viktor Frankl writes about being an inmate in a Nazi death camp. For him in that inhuman situation, laughter was his spiritual food. He and a fellow-inmate made a pact: Each day, they would find something—anything—to laugh about. With the perspective of humor, no matter what was happening on the physical level, there was a spiritual "sweet spot" that no brutality could conquer. To give you an idea of the "leverage" humor provided during those darkest moments, this is a joke that actually circulated among camp inmates:

Two Jewish guys decide to assassinate Hitler. They know his motorcade passes a certain intersection every day at 11:00 a.m., and so they are waiting for him. 11:00 a.m., and Hitler hasn't shown up. 11:15, 11:30, still no fuehrer. When the motorcade still hasn't arrived by 11:45, one of the would-be assassins turns to the other and says, "Gee, I hope nothing has happened to him."

This is not to say that humor is the only tool in the toolkit, or that it is always appropriate. We've all known people who have used humor as a shield (if not an actual weapon!) to keep others at arm's length, or to keep themselves from facing some of the difficult truths about their own lives and choices.

Ironically, there is a kind of soul nourishment that comes from being fully awake during times of suffering. But at some point, the suffering has served its useful purpose, and at that point laughter can help us lift the veil so we feel the full force (or should I say "full farce") of the Universe's love.

Now, who's to say what's really true? In fact, I read recently that even the Uncertainty Principle has been called into question! Beliefs are no more than choices, so it makes sense to believe that which creates healing and happiness. So that's why I subscribe to Swami Beyondananda's credo: "Life is a joke . . . but God is laughing with us, not at us."

for reflection

Here are some ideas in Steve's own words for implementing the ideas you read about in his essay. He suggests ten ways to bring more laughter to your life every day. Choose one to practice each day. You will soon feel yourself becoming lighter. You will be on the road to enlightenment.

TEN WAYS TO WAKE UP LAUGHING—
AND LEAVE LAUGHTER IN YOUR WAKE

1. Laugh every day. seriously . . . laughter is good for you. And when things "just aren't funny"—that's the most important time to laugh. Try this at home: Watch America's Funniest Home Videos with the sound off and Spike Jones playing instead.

2. Don't worry, you're already funny. Instead of trying to be funny, learn to see funny. Especially learn to see what's funny about you. Imagine God watching the Comedy Channel, and you are what's on.

3. Bring laughter to the outernet. Take the best of those jokes you get on the internet and share them on the "outernet." Practice by telling the same joke to five people. Short jokes are fine. Remember, it's not the length of the joke that matters, it's how much pleasure it gives.

4. Savor and save humorous healing stories. A good laughsitive cleanses the system and leaves the mind open to receive nourishment. Keep a notebook of jokes that "enlighten as they lighten." You will find yourself remembering and using them just at the right time.

5. Turn worry into laughter. When you find yourself worrying about something, step back from the worry and see if you can find something in the situation to laugh about. Worrying has no proven benefits. Laughter does. Did you know that one Youngman of laughter—the mirth contained in the average one-liner—can release up to a megahurt of emotional pain?

6. Reframe suffering as comedy in disguise. Sing the blues when you are angry, sad or frustrated. If you must complain, complain creatively—and thoroughly enjoy your complaining. Say, "You know what I love about this . . .?" Look for the comedy "hidden in this picture." (e.g., "I'm not on the verge of bankruptcy. I'm just having a near-debt experience.")

7. Build critical "muscle" by pumping ironies. Looking for the inherent contradictions and incongruities in situations helps build a strong body politic. Train your inner child to ask, "How come that emperor isn't wearing any clothes?" When you watch the news or read the papers, be on the lookout for signs of irony deficiency.

8. Develop a comic alter ego. A shy, mild-mannered man named Edgar Bergen went "inside" and found a brash, outrageous alter ego which he called Charlie McCarthy—who would do and say things that would make Edgar blush. Even if your "character" never makes it beyond your bathroom mirror, a comic alter ego is a great way to give voice to daily frustrations and lovingly laugh at your own "shadow." One of the best ways to break the addiction to your own personality is to try some other ones on!

9. Write your laugh story. Spend an afternoon or evening writing your life story as if it were a comedy. Which comic actors could play your family, friends, and foes? Who would you get to play your part? Give your story a title. A friend of mine calls his "Don't Do What I Did!"

10. Play regularly. Have you ever felt the Creator is toying with you? Well then, follow Swami Beyondananda's sage advice and become a creative plaything. Bring the childlike quality of play back into your life. Run up the down escalator. Dress for Halloween—any day the mood hits you. Plant the seeds of harmless fun wherever you go.

Living a conscious life

■ BARBARA DE ANGELIS, PH.D.

Dr. Barbara De Angelis expresses the truth about life, love, and relationships simply and clearly so that anyone, from a beginner on the journey to a seasoned spiritual seeker, receives an "Aha" from her words. Barbara's personal stories serve as examples of the principles she presents. She writes with the humility of a person who has walked the path, stumbled, fallen, gotten back up, learned something from the experience, and then moved on.

For the past twenty-five years, Barbara has been inspiring tens of millions of people throughout the world with her books, CDs, and television appearances. She is the author of more than fourteen best-selling books. Her first book, *How to Make Love All the Time*, was a national bestseller. She's been seen on *Oprah, The Today Show, Good Morning America,* and *The View.*

Barbara believes that people have misconceptions about spiritual growth: that one will never experience anger or have problems, and that everything will be perfect. She calls it "a magical thinking; a kind of kindergarten spirituality." This theme is amplified in her latest book, *How Did I Get Here? Finding Your Way to Renewed Hope and Happiness When Life and Love Take Unexpected Turns.*

In her essay, Barbara teaches that *how* we go through what happens to us is more important than *what* happens to us.

There's an old American Indian saying that when an eagle takes off from the ground, it never flies straight up like an airplane. It circles as it goes higher and higher and it keeps covering the same ground. I think that's the same for all of us. We all have x number of issues and it does feel, at times, like we're going over the same things over and over again. I think these are our life lessons and we have five, six, or ten courses we've signed up for in this life, and we will keep going through the same material. But each time, we do it from a higher vantage point. We recover more quickly, bring more wisdom, react with more love, and heal the pattern from a higher level. That's also an understanding I think it's important for people to have: sometimes when we see something familiar we say, "But, I thought I dealt with that." And we did, but now we're getting to deal with it in a different way.

Most of us believe that success is achieving the list of shoulds: I should have the right husband, I should have the right job, and I should weigh 120 pounds. Each person has his or her own list. At the end of each day, we look at that list in our minds, unconsciously, and we think, "How did I do?" And let's say we didn't make a sale, didn't have good clients, didn't sell the house, make a profit, or meet a deadline; we feel it was not a successful day. What we mean is, we didn't have a day that fits our expectations about success. Instead of defining success as what you've achieved or acquired, why not begin to define your success as how much you are growing each day. The purpose of life is to grow into the best human being you can be. If that's the case, then each day your main goal is to grow into the best human being you can be that day. And you have control over that no matter what happens on the outside. You can't control what's going to happen on any given day with the people you work with or with circumstances. But you can control how you deal with it.

For example, if you learn one new thing, it will be a successful day. If you've been patient with someone or yourself, it will be a successful day. I've had so many people tell me this has been such an eye-opening way of thinking. We all want to feel successful, but when we're basing our success on outer events; we're always going to be on a roller coaster ride, because 99 percent of those events are not under our control. The only way to take control is to take control of your inner feeling of success and to redefine what success means for you.

All growth requires change. And all change requires letting go. And letting go is usually painful. It's not that growth itself is painful, but the way we deal with the whole process is painful, because we tend to cling to our comfort zones. I think that not misinterpreting difficult times or painful times is one of the most important lessons on the spiritual path. We have to really know that pain causes us to wake up and pay immediate attention. Pain contains great liberation within it, but we, especially in our society because we're so into "feelgood," tend to think that if we're uncomfortable, we must be doing something wrong. Or if we're uncomfortable, something bad must be happening to us. This couldn't be further from the truth. Imagine a woman in labor; what if no one ever told her that labor was painful? What if she had this image of babies popping out and everyone being happy? She goes into labor and it's time for the baby to come out and all of a sudden it starts to hurt and she's screaming in agony, "Something terrible is happening to me. I'm dying. This is a nightmare. Help me." And now imagine what it would be like for her if another person came along and told her gently, "No dear, it's supposed to be painful. The pain is creating an opening for your child to come through." So then, she still doesn't like the pain, but she understands the purpose of the pain.

That's what we need to understand about growth in ourselves. Pain is an inevitable part of the growth process as we rebirth ourselves over and over again. And it doesn't necessarily mean that we are doing something wrong. Now, obviously if you're in a relationship with someone and he's abusing you, or you're in a job where you're being mistreated terribly, you don't say "pain is good for me." But, in many cases the discomfort we feel is just our ego being challenged, or our ego dying, or our old beliefs crumbling. And that's a good pain. It's the pain of rebirth.

Every situation is really just an opportunity for you to interact in a big seminar with the universe through all kinds of challenges. That's really all it is. It's not that you have to do that work or the universe is going to fall apart. It's just your vehicle for learning. We need to, if we can, detach ourselves enough to realize that, and not be so identified with, "Oh my God! I have to sell this many books or this many magazines." Success is what happens to your soul in the process of facing life's challenges.

We tend to judge things in our society in terms of quantity and volume. The people who are successful are the ones who sell the most records or make the most money. So, when we're doing things on a scale that doesn't look big to us, sometimes we think we're not making a difference. The truth is that that's really a way to rip ourselves off.

I remember when I wrote my first book, *How to Make Love All the Time*, I was very inexperienced as an author and I didn't quite know how to promote it. It was selling but it wasn't selling as well as I wanted it to. When I came back from my book tour and it hadn't become a bestseller, I was very despondent.

Then I met a couple who had flown from Florida to Los Angeles for one of my seminars. They came up to me during one of the breaks and said that they just wanted to tell me that they had read my book and it saved their marriage. They thanked me from the bottom of their hearts and then walked away. I could practically feel God with her/his arms folded saying, "Well, did you get the message?" I realized that I wrote the book for those people. It didn't matter who else read it. Touching two lives like that was really a precious thing.

Being in love means being in the state of love, not particularly being in love with a person or a thing, but being in a state of love, your own love. Allowing yourself to feel it, to drink it, and allowing yourself to then come out and be in that state with people you wouldn't ordinarily be in love with. I just had that experience today: I had to do some errands and did a whole bunch of little things like getting my driver's license renewed. I practiced feeling my own state of love and allowing others to see it and feel it. I had a remarkable morning because people really were responding to it. They were feeling very connected to me and I was feeling connected to them, and I hardly spoke to any of them. That experience is possible for all of us much more readily than we think.

Fear and love can't coexist, and we're choosing between them at every moment. If you're living in fear, you're going to be very devoid of love. You can be a prisoner to your fear. You have to take a look at how fear is holding you back in all areas of your life and slowly and compassionately move out of that. The truth is that the person who hurts us the most and holds us back the most is ourselves—nobody else—because we're misinterpreting our fear and we have to understand that fear is natural when we're really moving. If people aren't feeling any fear then they're usually pretty stuck. Fear makes us move and wake up from a state of inertia where there's no growth.

Really living a conscious life means bringing all of the tools, all of the beliefs, all of the lessons you learned to each situation, and, to the best of your ability, up-leveling your relationships and up-leveling the way you treat your body. It also means up-leveling your relationship to your work, your money, to everything. It really is a lot of work. The unspoken secret of the seeker is that she feels sometimes she was doing better before she went on a spiritual path. Then the truth hits her that she has to go and clean up this and that. And you know what? You do! But the rewards are tremendous. The most important thing is bringing these core values, these spiritual secrets into your daily life and remembering that the obstacles are here to teach you. It's also about remembering that the people you encounter are your teachers. When you take all these things and apply them, you create a constant arena for your spiritual growth.

for reflection

For Barbara De Angelis being in love is really being in a state of love . . . an attitude that heals the planet. This is a wonderful way to make a contribution to the world in a very impersonal way.

How do we get to be in a state of love? Love is a thought. This thought is in all of us . . . in the depths of our bodies, minds, and souls. We are so caught up in worldly things that we forget that the energy that drives the universe is the energy of love. Another way to think about this idea is simply to allow your light to shine.

Let's practice allowing our light to shine. To generate our light, it doesn't matter where we are. Just imagine the glow of a firefly deep inside your belly and see it joined by a thousand other fireflies. Its light is getting warmer and brighter. Allow the light to warm your abdomen, then pulse through your chest and exit your head in all directions, warming everyone you can possibly see. This is an act of unconditional love and you'll find that people will "get it." Some responses will be more evident than others, but again the greatest beneficial effect of thinking these thoughts are for you. Love is in inexhaustible resource. The more you give away the more you generate. Love is an inexhaustible resource. This simple exercise will leave you feeling lighter, happier, and relaxed.

Revealing your true beauty

■ LARRY DUBITSKY

Larry Dubitsky is a born teacher. He has the ability to spark the creative spirit in students from age five to seventy-five. Larry has written prolifically and lectured extensively on both spiritual topics and artistic principles. He has been a student and teacher of A Course in Miracles since 1977. He has taught countless Course groups over the years. In his role as art teacher, he has given lectures on the topics of figure drawing, watercolor techniques and picture composition to many art groups both in New York and Florida.

Larry believes that at the core of every person is an infinite well of creativity just waiting to be revealed. Spiritual living is about the willingness to remove the masks of self-doubt that hide it.

A mask is a false self-image that lies both to you and to the world. Some people wear a mask of victimization. Other people wear masks of detachment. Others wear masks that reflect the trappings of a group, class, or ideology with which they identify. As you wander from one social scene to another you might find cowards using macho masks and people of prejudice creating masks of welcome. The mask becomes the presentation of our persona to the outside world. Unfortunately, sometimes the persona we present to others is not the persona we really are.

Why do we wear masks? The answer is simple. Many of us feel we are not good enough, smart enough, and nobody likes us. So, we create a fiction. The mask hides who we really are. We really are good enough, smart enough and likable, because our essence is love. But we don't believe that. We don't believe that we are innocent, holy children of God, worthy of love, respect, and acceptance, because of who we naturally are.

Most masks are not held firmly in place; sometimes they slip. In the TV show *Keeping Up Appearances,* Hyacinth, the main character, tries to wear an upper-class mask, but it doesn't fit well; it keeps giving way to the tugs of her lower-class family's soap operas. We laugh. A lot of comedy describes mask slippage, or loss of face as it is more commonly called.

I was invited to a Salon not long ago. The idea of a Salon is to create a gathering of people who have common interests. They gather together to share ideas. Refreshments were served and then we sat down for serious talks. The rules were very simple. We all took turns and each person was given two minutes to tell the group why they had come to the Salon this night. Each person talked without interruption, and then a general discussion began.

During the two minute introductory talk that each person gave, the masks were held on tightly. They seemed to fit well; they were very convincing. But during the general discussion, however, emotions were stirred deeply within most of the participants. Some of the masks started slipping; others fell off onto the floor and were quickly picked up and put back on again. Others exploded from the inside out. Inner emotional spasms threw one mask against a wall (figuratively) and shattered it into many pieces. The mask was irretrievable. This person spent the remainder of the evening trying to make another mask, one that would bolster his image and also convince others that he was really a pussycat. He spent a lot of time trying to erase the image of the hyena that emerged when his mask disintegrated.

It was a very interesting experience to see people present themselves to a group as one kind of person, and then in the heat of argument become another. One of them was a "goody two shoes," who metamorphosed into a lioness. Another, whose mask was that of a wise, dignified, kindly person, acted like a bumbling fool when personally attacked.

Most of the world has an inferiority complex. We are taught incessantly that we have to do better today then we did yesterday, and we have to do better tomorrow than we did today. Few people believe they are good enough just the way they are.

All of us, at one time or another, have met people who have thrown away their masks. They are spontaneous, loving and happy. They have accepted themselves as they are and live in a state of "Being." Their company is joyous and inspirational. The only difference between them and us is that they know they are good enough, smart enough and likable.

for reflection

When you let go of your masks, you reveal your inner beauty. The steps for letting go of your masks are simple but not easy.

Think of some people you know well. How many of these people use a mask that does not reflect their true nature? Are you willing to allow your true nature to be seen by everyone, regardless of their relationship to you? If you are, you are ready to let go of your mask.

Make yourself comfortable. Visualize the mask you use in everyday life. What does it look like? What is it you are trying to hide? How much energy are you putting into holding on to your mask? A mask that's designed to protect you in some way keeps you in a state of fear. It also prevents you from experiencing real intimacy, love and sharing.

Self-talk is the most important talk there is. You are the most important person you can possibly talk to. Take a deep breath, and relax. Relax, relax, relax. Feel the rhythm of your innermost being. Listen to the music of your soul. Some spiritual teachers say that the soul is a tiny point of light that is located right behind your forehead. Can you imagine a point of light there? Allow that light to grow larger and larger and larger until it fills your entire head and expands to fill your neck, torso, arms, and legs. You are now a beautiful being of shining light. Know that you are perfect, because God made you, and God does not make mistakes. Allow your inner light to shine. See this light energize and inspire all those around you, all those dear to your heart.

Now open your eyes and remember this. You need no mask because you are a radiant child of God, just as you are.

Authenticity

■ DEBBIE FORD

To meet Debbie Ford is to be warmed by the light that shines from her smile. She is peace personified. Her mission, as expressed on her web site, is to inspire "humanity to lead fully integrated lives." That mission statement reflects Debbie's own life as well as her teachings. She has explored the fullness of her own humanity, including her own darkness. Her best-selling book, *The Dark Side of the Light Chasers,* is an honest, gentle exploration of how to take into ourselves those parts of us that we have judged to be less than perfect. The result is easier acceptance of our own and everyone else's imperfections, but more than that, our creativity is uncovered. We face the fear that has obscured our brilliance. And our lights get brighter, just like Debbie's.

Debbie's essay focuses on how to access our divinity and use it as a tool to grow through our humanity.

Much of my path has been about cleansing my consciousness. Cleansing your consciousness provides you with a clean slate. We carry around so much unresolved stuff from our past that it creates a filter.

The first step in cleansing your consciousness is to go in and see what is unresolved from the past: What beliefs have we created that would prevent us from living a spiritual life? What disempowering or negative thoughts are we still thinking?

These thoughts cause us to repeat patterns over and over again. They are the shadow beliefs that drive our behavior and are part of our unconscious masks. They drive what we say, what we think, what we do, and how we express ourselves.

It's easy to live a spiritual life when there are no hidden agendas. When you are willing to give up your will, and are able to identify your will as the same will of the universe, God, or however you refer to divine intelligence. The more your consciousness is cleared of the past, the easier it becomes to live in accord with the divinity.

Learning to recognize the differences between our humanity and our divinity takes practice. How do we know when we're in our humanity or in our divinity? Our ego is a part of our humanity. Our ego is there to protect us and to set us apart from others. One exercise that will help you identify the difference is to look at what you are trying to get everybody to think or believe about you. This exercise will help you discover the beliefs you grew up with that you're still harboring. It helps you see what patterns you keep repeating and what beliefs actually drive these patterns. If we're willing to explore the thoughts and feelings of our humanity, then we can distinguish between those times when we're standing in our divinity, because when we're standing in our divinity our minds are quiet. That is the best way to tell. It's peaceful in there. It's quiet; there are no thoughts of right, wrong, good, or bad. You stop beating yourself up with self-doubt and self-criticism.

For many people who are on a spiritual path, there is a resistance from their ego. Many spiritual teachings are worded in such a way that they would make you believe that the ego is bad. As soon as we call anything bad or pass judgment on it, we have created resistance to it. What we resist expands. Only the ego would have you get rid of the ego. The Divine wouldn't have you get rid of the ego. We're divinely created and so we're created with an ego. If you don't have a strong ego or any ego at all, then you can't distinguish yourself from others and you'd probably end up in a mental hospital. We need to honor all of our divinity, which includes our humanity. Divinity is ultimately about self-forgiveness. It is about forgiving ourselves for being human, forgiving ourselves for being flawed, and forgiving ourselves for being a work in progress.

Self-forgiveness helps us see that even our shadow sides have positive value. For example, anger can help you set boundaries or can help you find your passion. Anger and passion go hand in hand. Anger can help you make changes in the world. I wouldn't do what I do if I weren't so angry that people don't love themselves, but need to learn to love all parts of themselves. Anger and even bitchiness are part of my humanity. If I hate them, then I hate myself. Then I hate the God within. You can't hate yourself, or parts of yourself, and think that you're in alignment with your divine self.

All we have to do is ask ourselves if there was a God looking down, would she tell us that we're bad or wrong, or say, "You shouldn't be like that"?

Our human parts can serve a purpose. It doesn't mean that it's okay to use your anger or bitchiness against other people. To love, honor, and embrace our humanity doesn't mean you can become abusive. On the other hand, some people don't want to get angry because their anger hurt them in the past. But when used appropriately, anger is a sacred emotion.

To cleanse yourself of anger consciously, you can begin by asking yourself, "What am I really am angry about?" Generally it's old anger and old wounds or something from the past for which we have not forgiven ourselves. But sometimes we get angry because we really need to stand up for ourselves. In that case, we're adding to our life force. If a person is living with someone who is critical and abusive, a dose of anger saying "you are not allowed to do that to me" is healthy. Some people need to learn to use anger to their benefit and to stand up for themselves; other people need to confront and heal it because they use it against other people. Neither is really better than the other. There are lessons to be learned in each part of ourselves.

Sometimes it's painful to look at the ego. For most of us it is painful to look at anything other than the ideal that our society offers us, which is the idea of a good person. I love what Carl Jung said: "I would rather be whole than good." That is so powerful. Most people are trying to be good people. That means that whatever was thought to be good in the society in which you grew up, if you weren't "that," then you were bad. My work is really about going in and challenging and questioning that. It's about integrating what we think are the bad parts of ourselves. It is deep work and for some people it can be painful. I always say that it is more painful to live with hating or not liking yourself, or not creating a future you desire because you have some unresolved issues that you're not willing to confront. It's more painful to go to your grave knowing that you haven't expressed your greatest self.

We have within us a spiritual source that can help us confront that pain. When we're in pain and we connect with our spiritual selves and say, "I don't know how to handle this. I don't know how to get through this. Please show me you're there. Please give me the courage—just for today, or just for this hour—to get through this," then we're using our divinity. Part of the process is convincing our humanity and our ego that it's safe to live from the Source of our Being and express our divinity. That's how I started; hour by hour and day by day. Then, I paid attention and watched how things began to unfold more smoothly and make more sense. I saw how much God was in my life and how much I was supported. I noticed how many times I thought I couldn't make it, but I did. Acknowledging that builds up trust. Surrendering to God, divinity, or whatever you want to call it is only about trusting in the good of the universe. It's trusting that everything that comes into our awareness is there to help serve, benefit, and heal us. If we trust in that, then we can really get through anything.

for reflection

Debbie Ford tells us that to live life fully, we have to accept all parts of ourselves, including our shadow sides. These are aspects of ourselves that are not always pleasant but often useful. This bundle of parts is sometimes called the ego. The idea here is not to get rid of these ego traits, like ambition, drawing boundaries, displaying anger or fear, but rather to use them appropriately.

For example, anger is very useful when someone tries to use you as a doormat. Ambition will bring us financial security and well-being, and defining boundaries helps give us a sense self-worth and privacy.

Make yourself comfortable. Close your eyes. Feel yourself going down deeper and deeper. You have reached the cellar of your mind. Carefully search through the recesses of the basement. There it is . . . in a far corner, your musty old memory chest. Open it. Look through the old memories. Pick an incident where you know you used anger inappropriately, or where you misdirected your anger. Say this aloud, so that you can hear your own voice clearly: "I ask for forgiveness for myself for using anger inappropriately." Allow the incident to be erased from your mind.

Now take a deep breath. Let it out slowly. Pick another happening from your memory box. This one is about using ambition inappropriately. Ambition can be used inappropriately when it is used for self-aggrandizement or to dominate, manipulate, or hurt others. Say this aloud, so that you can hear your own voice clearly "I ask for forgiveness for myself for using ambition inappropriately." Allow the happening to be erased from your mind.

Continue this exercise on a daily basis, until your mind is cleared and at peace. Know that the cleared mind is a compassionate mind, a healing mind able to extend peace and love in abundance, a whole mind able to use ego skills whenever necessary.

health
& healing

Healing

■ CAROLINE MYSS, PH.D.

These days, of all the teachers and lecturers out on the circuit marketing their transformational wares, Caroline Myss's teachings rank among the most truly transformational. Myss offers "boot camp spirituality." She honestly tells her millions of fans that growth and healing are not easy. She prods and cajoles us to wake up and take responsibility for our own lives. Everything that happens to us, she teaches, happens because of Divine appointment and by our choice. It is a teaching that at times is a bitter pill to swallow, and yet, as she would say, "How else are our souls going to evolve and blossom into their full potential?"

Myss has a Ph.D. in Intuition and Energy Medicine, as well as an M.A. in Theology and a B.A. in Journalism. She has co-founded the Language of Intuition Program and, the Institute for the Science of Medical Intuition. Her best-selling books include *Why People Don't Heal and How They Can* and *Anatomy of the Spirit*. Although she is no longer in practice as a medical intuitive, she uses the same laser beam focus of mind in her teaching so that every word conveys precisely the exact message she means to convey. The result is a teaching that is profoundly deep and profoundly healing.

When a person takes chemical medicine, passive belief processes are more engaged than active ones. It is assumed that you don't have to do anything, and that the medicine will do all the work. You cannot have that assumption with energy medicine; it simply doesn't work that way. When you talk about conscious medicine versus passive medicine, the fact is that with conscious medicine, you to do your own inner work; you have to consciously participate, and that makes a big difference.

Most people don't know what it means to heal bitterness, for example. There has to be willingness to go that extra emotional, psychological, and spiritual distance, to confront your own bitterness at an energetic level. Many people aren't willing to do that. Think of energy medicine as being most effective in preserving time. You have to be emotionally and spiritually present to be able to engage it in its fullest force. If you are consumed with anger, it's not just anger; it's disappointment, frustration, or some other emotion about the past. You're consumed with your history. And it's not just that either, it's also that you are psychically and emotionally undisciplined.

Living in appreciation of your life—as it is right now—is also required for healing. It means that you don't live in the place of would-have-could-have-should-have-been. You live in the idea that there is something good about your life every day, which should be fueled with your passion, and not diluted by your lack of appreciation for all the good that's happening in your life right now. That kind of awareness is foreign for many people.

Energy medicine stimulates your psyche and your spirit. There are many methods that could be classified as energy medicine, from meditation to laying on of hands, acupressure, and therapeutic touch.

Breath work and yoga should not be classified as medicine or as energy treatments. There is a difference between practices and treatments, which should be clearly understood. In the western model, they have turned these practices it into self-treatment, which is inappropriate. Yoga is a spiritual practice, and meditation is a spiritual practice; they are not health techniques. That they happen to help you maintain your health is a side blessing, but they are, make no mistake, spiritual practices, and should be honored as that.

Energy treatments will of course continue to develop. You can be sure that vibrational medicine will come into play with more and more uses of color and sound. Everything is energy first and matter second. We now live in a culture in which our primary language has become energy and it's called the Internet. We have become a species that communicates solely through energy. Who in the world writes letters anymore? The Internet is very much a physical manifestation of what could be thought of as the global brain, or the spiritual brain. We have duplicated the instantaneous way we have always communicated with each other. We have finally proved that thoughts travel instantaneously. We can influence and affect the globe—the entire globe—in one thought. A computer virus changes the shape of the world with one push of the button. We have finally created a system that reflects a spiritual truth at its basic or mundane form. Learning about the potency of thought is reshaping the way that we treat people. Now we are treating people with therapy that is energy treatment.

Spirituality is a discipline that is the maintenance and the evolution of the shadow in all of us. That's what it is about. When you look at all spiritual disciplines, why do you think

they emphasize forgiveness? Because bitterness and vengefulness are so easy, and so natural; forgiveness is not natural, it
requires effort. Vengefulness is natural. The whole idea of spirituality is to make the spirit stronger than the natural instinct.

for reflection

*Chemical medicine is based on the assumption that the
patient is passive and only the drug you ingest is active. In energy
medicine the opposite is true. All healing activity is generated by
the patients themselves; the intermediary, or healer, is just there to
help direct the energy of the patient.*

*Caroline Myss, along with Louise Hay and many others,
believe that hurtful emotions cause illness. In order to lead a
healthy life, they believe you have to rid yourself of your negative
emotions. The task of the energy healer is to help you do this, but
make no mistake about it, you are the one doing the work.*

*Appreciation and gratitude for your present life and circum-
stances, letting go of hatred, anger, and feelings of victimization are
essential for leading a healthy life.*

*Be still a moment, take a deep breath. Close your eyes and
see your present life in your mind's eye. Think of all the good feelings you have known, think of all the pleasures you are blessed
with right now. Just be still a while and let things happen, and if
any disturbing thought comes to mind take the magic pen that you
find in your right hand and cross it out with a big red X. See the
thought crumple and fall into the void; allow this to happen as long
as necessary. Then open your eyes and wake up refreshed.*

Reinventing medicine

■ LARRY DOSSEY, M.D.

Dr. Larry Dossey is a physician of internal medicine who strives to anchor the holistic health movement in a medical model that is scientifically respectable and that, at the same time, answers people's inner spiritual needs. Throughout his career Dr. Dossey has tended several professional posts, including chief of staff at Medical City Dallas Hospital and co-chair of the Panel on Mind/Body Interventions, Office of Alternative Medicine, National Institutes of Health. He was executive editor of the journal *Alternative Therapies in Health and Medicine* for nearly a decade. Through his groundbreaking research that weaves science and spirit, Dr. Dossey has become a sought-after speaker and author. His book *Healing Words: The Power of Prayer and the Practice of Medicine* was a *New York Times* bestseller, followed by the groundbreaking book *Reinventing Medicine*. Larry and his colleagues have recently launched a new journal, *EXPLORE: The Journal of Science and Healing*, which continues his mission of creating a medical model that is grounded in both science and spirit.

In this essay, Dr. Dossey continues the discussion of spirituality's positive role in science by revealing the latest advances in what he calls Era III medicine.

Era III medicine is best seen in context with Eras I and II. Let me give a quick background. Since medicine first began to be scientific, beginning around the middle of the 1800s, we can make out three main periods. The first period, Era I, is mechanical medicine because it revolves around physical things such as drugs, surgical procedures, irradiation, and so on. Era II or mind-body medicine began to develop one hundred years later in the 1950s, and focuses on using your own thoughts and emotions to change your personal health: meditation, relaxation-guided imagery, hypnosis, and so on. Era III medicine, which we have recently entered, is the latest development. These eras are not exclusive and they overlap, of course, but nonetheless are distinctive.

Era III medicine suggests that you can use your own thoughts to change not just your own body—that's Era II— but also somebody else's. This invokes what I call nonlocal mind. Nonlocal is just a fancy term for "infinite." It implies the ability of consciousness to cause changes in the world outside your body. Era III medicine suggests, for instance, that distant intercessory prayer, or remote healing, is real and that we should take seriously the scientific evidence and controlled studies showing this. So Era III medicine comes into play anytime consciousness manifests outside your body, out there in the world. And the reason for putting forward this contention is simple: it's data. There are scores of studies that compel us to advance Era III as a possibility.

Robert Sapolsky, an eminent geneticist, has provided profound insights into Era II, the domain in which your mind can affect your own body in healthful ways. In an article for *Newsweek* a few years ago, called "It's Not All in the Genes," Sapolsky described how there are many factors that modify what our genes do. The point is that they are not absolute dictators, as many people believe. One of the factors that influences them is consciousness. For example, there is a genetic disorder called fish-skin disease, a horrible problem in which the skin becomes alligator-like, cracked, infected, and fissured. There's no known physical cure. However, five cases of this serious genetic disorder have now been published in which the problem was cured or dramatically improved with hypnosis. So here you have an example, documented in medical science, that your consciousness can dramatically change what your genes do. The lesson is that "the physical" is not everything; consciousness also gets in on the act.

But we should be careful and not think that consciousness actually changes our genes. That's going too far. But what we sure as heck do know is that consciousness changes how our genes behave. Thus, it's not only the environment and the food you eat that change the activity of your genes, but also your consciousness, the love and touch you get from your parents and others in life, and so on. You can make a long list of these modifying influences. Consciousness is just one of them.

Now perhaps you try Era III medicine to effect change through your consciousness and find that nothing seems to happen. Does this mean that Era III medicine should be disregarded? And should you blame yourself for doing something wrong if you see no results? Should you feel guilty? Let's remember, we don't get down on penicillin just because it has nearly a 50 percent failure rate in treating strep throat. So why should we blame consciousness or prayer, for example, because they aren't 100 percent effective? It's an amazing thing; we rush to blame ourselves, our mind, thought patterns, and cells, but we let other things that don't work all the time off the hook. I mean, there isn't any therapy that's 100 percent effective. Why should we demand that our consciousness operate with total effectiveness in preventing or curing illness? It's totally irrational. So we need to work on what I've called New-Age guilt and not beat up on our own consciousness so often.

There's an epidemic of this kind of guilt in our culture. As an internist, I used to counsel patients frequently who would come to me with these shame-and-blame issues. Many of them were raised in strict religious traditions, and they felt like spiritual failures. I would advise them to get a book on the lives of the saints and read about the health histories of some of the greatest religious figures in history. Often they were wrecks. So here are people who were very close to God, who presumably had gorgeous spiritual lives, yet they developed serious health problems. There's a lesson there. It's not the case that spiritual perfection always goes hand in hand with good physical health. That's really a hot button for me, because I know there are lots of teachers out there who preach to high heaven that if you're just spiritual enough, evolved enough, or enlightened enough, you won't get sick. That's bad biology; it's bad psychology; it's bad spirituality. There's no proof for that. I call it metaphysical malpractice. If you pray and heart disease improves, that's wonderful. But that's not the main benefit of prayer. Prayer's main purpose is to help us connect with the Absolute, the Transcendent, or whatever term we place on that.

I have a lot of colleagues in the New Age movement. I stand up for them because they began with a profound insight:

that consciousness is important. It really does make a difference in the world. But be careful if you permit your individual consciousness to become all-important, as just a tool with which you can manipulate the world. People lose their balance when they become too enthusiastic about something, no matter what it is. The field of alternative medicine is just filled with that. But so, too, is modern medicine.

for reflection

We live in a time where all the Eras of medicine that Dr. Dossey describes can be seen operating simultaneously: medication, surgery, positive thinking, and prayer. But it's usually our first inclination to rely solely on Era I medicine and to place our hopes in the power of traditional forms of medicine such as pills, operations, drugs, and shots. But, what if we also explored "the most revolutionary" Era, Era III, and investigated whether it really works. Dr. Dossey believes it does. What if we took up his charge that Era III medicine does create positive change in external circumstances through our consciousness? Think of all the healing that could take place. Think of all the lives that could be changed.

Let's give it a shot. Is there someone you know who could use some healing? Maybe you have a neighbor who is suffering from cancer. Maybe there's someone at work who's trapped in depression. Think of someone whose life you want to positively impact by channeling positive energy towards them. Imagine their wound or ailment healing. Imagine their spirit being lifted. Imagine them smiling because they're no longer sick.

Change can happen. And it's up to you to give it a jump start.

Aging with purpose

■ RABBI CHAIM RICHTER

Rabbi Chaim Richter, at age seventy-eight, describes himself as a hedonistic altruist. He worked as a chaplain for South Broward Jewish Federation for twenty-five years before his retirement. He brings to his chaplaincy an eclectic mix of Judaism, meditation, gestalt therapy, the latest information on health and wellness, and a passion for singing and playing the guitar. He has touched the lives of many people in the South Florida community through organizations like Gestalt-in-Action (which he founded), a networking group for therapists and others interested in humanistic-type and psychospiritual therapies, as well as through an assortment of spiritual-growth oriented workshops he's presented at condo-communities, synagogues, and Jewish Community Centers in conjunction with the Spiritual Eldering Project. Rabbi Richter is also one of the founders of the Jewish AIDS Network.

He was raised in a joyous, centrist-Orthodox Jewish family in Chicago that fostered a deeply spiritual identity. In Yeshiva he experienced *devekut,* or cleaving to God in song and prayer. His interest in human potential sprang from years of self-seeking through therapy and his involvement in the human potential movement. Rabbi Richter also has a Master's degree in Counseling Psychology and is a Florida Licensed Mental Health Counselor.

Rabbi Richter's spiritual studies include meditation, Tai Chi, yoga, Kabbalah, *A Course in Miracles,* kundalini energy work, Spiritual Eldering, and death and dying.

These days, Rabbi Richter says he is slowing down. That means he no longer runs 12 to 18 miles a week, but he still plays tennis and regularly practices Chi Gong and Tai Chi. He is still conducting bereavement groups, spiritual eldering classes, and healing circles.

My father was a very compassionate man. During World War II, he was only making $25 a week and supporting a family of four kids and a wife. Yet he still gave 20 percent out of his $25 to a week to *tzedakah* (charity). Whenever he saw someone who needed help-an old man, a widow, somebody who was in need-he would pull a dollar or two out of his pocket.

I got involved in the AIDS movement because in 1989 I met a woman whose son had died of AIDS. She told me that she didn't know any Rabbis whom she felt she could talk to and from whom she could receive comfort. Then and there I decided this was my mission, and within a month, I started an AIDS group with Jewish Family Service. I found I was a pioneer in the field. I spent four years giving up my Wednesday nights without compensation to lead a group. Today there is a Jewish AIDS Network. I no longer have to expend as much energy now that other people are taking a more active part.

However, I must bear in mind that the stress of my many ventures sometimes overwhelms me. About twelve years ago, I suffered from a TIA, a mild stroke. That caused me to change my life style. I went on the Zone diet. I researched it thoroughly and contacted the author of *The Zone*, Barry Sears. I have a propensity for healthy living. I take vitamins and Chinese herbs, undergo acupuncture therapy, and meditate.

When someone comes to me seeking advice on how to attain inner peace, I advise meditation. Meditation has many faces. There could be hundreds of kinds of meditation. But it's a very personal thing. Inner peace is a state of Being. I have given talks to groups of people, some in their eighties, and I teach them the song:

> *Lord I want to do for You*
> *Lord I want to feel for You*
> *Lord I want to know for You*
> *Lord I want to be for You*

I describe Being as the place where I find peace. I find peace by going to the beach and sitting at the ocean's edge watching the waves coming in and going out. I also find peace when I'm *davenning* (praying), and when I meditate.

When I give classes, I give people a whole series of meditations, but they have to find their own way. Each person has to find his or her own way.

To me, spirituality is discovering that rock of the unknown in us. The Kabbalah describes four worlds; the worlds of action, feeling, knowledge, and being. A person who is very religious, *glatt* kosher for instance, well that person is operating on the level of level of *assiyah*, or action. The world of feelings is called *yetzirah*. Yetzirah is expressed in the intention (fervor or *kavvanah*) in your prayers. Then there's the world of knowledge called *briyah*, which the analytical knowledge of the Talmud. Briyah is also found in the spiritual, or creative knowledge that is found in the Kabbalah and in Hasidic tales. Beyond that is *atzilut*, the fourth world. That's a difficult one to describe. I felt it at certain rare moments when I deeply experienced a Oneness with God and humanity.

I'm slowly giving up different activities. Some time ago I began to savor the experience of Being. I just spent eleven days with Devera, my wife of forty years, at Vanderbilt Beach in Naples in total Being. We had a great time. We hardly went any-place; we just got into being, and we had a little beer. I'm slow-ly integrating the four worlds of action, feeling, knowledge, and Being into my way of life. That's what spirituality is: get-ting the four worlds all integrated with each other, just as my hedonism mingles with my altruism. I believe we're meant to have a good time on earth, and that is how I'm living my life.

for reflection

Chaim Richter dedicated his life to service to his varied communities. Many others believe that a life of service is a way to enlightenment. Ram Dass, Elisabeth Kübler Ross, Martin Luther King, Mohandas Gandi and Mother Teresa have all trod this path of service in their own unique way.

A good way to start on this path is to start with little things like just picking up a piece of paper in a public hallway and placing it in a trash can. The motivation for this act is simply to make the environment a better place for everyone to live in. Other people will be inspired by these simple acts of caring.

A businessman wanted to donate thousands of dollars to Mother Teresa's work. She refused to accept his donation unless

*he would spend a few days working with her. She felt it was impor-
tant for him to experience service in addition to donating to charity.*

*He came and served and his life was never the same after-
ward. He had what the psychologist Abraham Maslow called a peak
experience. His attitudes shifted and life became more fulfilling.*

*Acts of service, compassion for others, helping those in need
are stepping stones on the spiritual path to enlightenment.*

changing
the world

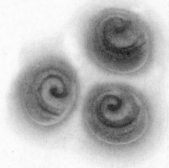

The world needs mothering

■ MA JAYA SATI BHAGAVATI

Ma Jaya Sati Bhagavati is an improbable Guru. Born into a poor Jewish family in Brooklyn, Ma Jaya made friends with the homeless who lived under the boardwalk of Coney Island. They taught her that there are no "throw-away" people. That spirit of caring for others is the life force that fuels Ma Jaya and Kashi Ashram, a center she founded in Sebastian, Florida, in 1976. Through this center, Ma Jaya and her volunteers provide food, friendship, and love to care center residents and people living with HIV/AIDS and other life-threatening illnesses, including foster children with chronic illnesses. They also sustain an orphanage in Uganda.

As a highly respected world spiritual leader, Ma Jaya is a trustee in the Governing Council of the Parliament of the World's Religions and is the founder of World Tibet Day. The Dalai Lama and Bishop Desmond Tutu have praised her work and admire Kashi's mission to "awaken a profound awareness about one's spiritual self and the issues that face the world today . . . an awakened soul is a catalyst that can change the world." And, to Ma Jaya, these aren't just words; they are her words in action.

In her essay, Ma Jaya reveals the importance of serving and reaching out to humanity. The world is full of people in need. It is when we are in tune with Spirit that we realize the magnitude of the need and how we must address it.

There are many ways of serving. One way we serve is through prayer, but how long can we keep our hands together? At some point, our hands have to touch someone, because so many have a fevered head that needs the cool touch of one who serves. Service is part of humanity's original nature. The Great Force, the magnetic field that calls us to serve, is not outside of us, but deep within our heart. It's a pattern we take with us from lifetime to lifetime. When we don't use it, it accumulates and it puts a lot of pressure on the human heart. It creates a feeling of emptiness. If we do not give to another human being, that which must be given away stagnates. The heart of life is that which we can give to another human being.

By giving of *yourself* to another human being, you release certain vibrations inside yourself. You become the Great Mother, because you are using that which must be used in honor of humanity. Service is not about religion. My God, it's not even about spirituality. One and one equals two. If the child is hungry, the mother feeds it. It's that simple. If the child is cold, the mother covers him or her. Male or female, when you serve, you become the Mother.

We have 900 children in my orphanage in Uganda. It is run by a magnificent priest, Father Centurio. This man literally takes abandoned children off the streets. There is so much horror there. There are starving people in America, but in Uganda, you have grandmas and you have grandchildren. The mothers and fathers are gone. A whole generation got wiped out because of AIDS or civil war. I had to do more than just watch it on TV and talk about it.

People come to Kashi Ashram from all over the world and ask why we don't burn out. The answer is simple. We drink as we pour; we pour as we drink. We keep moving the current of service (*seva*) through our own selves and bring it out into the world. Serving also brings great joy. But you don't think about that in the moment. In the moment, you don't think, "Well this is making me happy!'" You think, "I got a smile out of that kid. I got a twinkle in the eye of that child who is fighting AIDS or cancer." And you say, "Thank you, God, for letting me do this." I wish there wasn't all this pain in the world, but each of has the ability to make life a little bit better for someone else. You don't have to do what I do. You know when you have a big heart, something must fill it up. Caring is so deep in your heart that it must come out. It can be anything. Giving compliments to people is a form of service. When I see a beautiful woman or a handsome man, I'll stop and tell them.

Give away what you want the most for yourself. When I go into hospitals or into a county home, the first thing I tell myself is: "Okay, Ma, you're in that bed. What do you want in this moment?" Most people are afraid of the sick. Most people are afraid to touch a homeless person. You don't have to touch them, but there's never a reason not to smile. I learned that as a very young girl when my Mom was dying in a charity ward in Coney Island Hospital in Brooklyn. On her deathbed, my Mom would tell me to go around the ward and make people laugh. I was eight or nine years old at the time, and I did what my Mother told me. I ran around the ward and made everybody laugh. When I told her what I had done, she said, "Who did you touch with your own hand?" I said, "Nobody, Mom, nobody, but I made them all laugh." She said, "Now you go and you hug and you touch." I said, "But Mommy, they stink." And my Mom said, "So do I." That was my first lesson in total service and giving everything I have of myself. And I never tire. I cry a lot, but I never tire.

There are Native American Indian tribes that do not have a word for "me." They only have a word for "we." The earth is in great need of mothering. All one has to do to become the mother is to recognize that "we" is more important than "me." Women are coming to the forefront of the battle for humanity's needs, but this is the moment for all of us to remember that one does not have to have breasts filled with milk or a womb that once was full to be a mother; one only has to have a mother's heart. When one embraces the spirit of the mother, then there is no difference between a man's heart and a woman's heart. The earth needs nourishment. A feminine touch must be felt or this great, great Mother Earth is doomed. All of us must share the responsibility of alleviating the suffering that is occurring on this planet that is also so abundant. Anybody can get involved. Tell yourself, "I'll give a week; I'll give a day. I'll give an hour, or perhaps I'll just talk to somebody as a hotline volunteer." It's not about money, although money is desperately needed. As I said before, it's about what you are willing to give of yourself.

You're in prison if you don't take care of another human being. How much time do we need to sit in prayer to take care of ourselves? I teach a sacred yoga called Kali Natha Yoga that is going out all over the world. It combines movement with prayer and worship. It allows for a feeling of health, vitality, and deep inner peace. But it comes right down to this: when there are people who are hurt and you are someone who is capable of stopping that hurt, you have to take responsibility. It's not that God doesn't answer prayers. She, the Mother, looks down upon us all and says, "Take care of my children."

for reflection

Ma Jaya Sati Bhagavati's expression of spiritual living is the path of service. She knows that giving of yourself, in any way that is applicable in the moment, actually serves to enrich you. And, as Ma Jaya says, serving does not mean sacrificing. When you sacrifice, you are actually cut off from the Spirit. If you feel as though you are sacrificing, it means that you aren't taking time to nourish yourself. You feel deprived rather than fulfilled.

Have you ever served another with no thought of reward, or expectations and found a feeling of profound grace in the moment?

Opportunities for serving are all around us. Sometimes it's as simple as a gentle smile, a pat on the back, or a loving thought. Even a seemingly small gesture of kindness is enough to free another from fear and desperation. Try it wherever you are. Smile at the supermarket checkout cashier, for example. Or smile at the people around you while you're waiting in line at the movies. Ask your waitress whether she's having a good day.

Being in the service Spirit is easy. It's allowing your original nature to flow through you.

A public proposal

■ ALAN COHEN

Alan Cohen has been gracing the spiritual/self-help arena for well over twenty years. His books and tapes have inspired millions of people. His early books, *The Dragon Doesn't Live Here Anymore* and *Rising in Love*, were instant hits. Combining warmth, wit and wisdom, Alan touches people's hearts. He reminds readers to be gentle with themselves. The quote that most characterizes Alan's teachings is "angels can fly because they take themselves lightly."

Alan's books are filled with rich stories that focus on finding the miraculous in life's daily events. His stories bring spirituality down to earth. Reading an Alan Cohen book, listening to a tape, or, even better, taking one of his workshops, is like spending time with your best friend. With great compassion for the human condition, he encourages and empowers people to go within and connect to their soul. His methodology can be called "gentle transformation," meaning that people are able to move through life's challenges without the self-recrimination style of today's Dr. Phil generation.

In the following essay, Alan describes how a "sincere expression of love" is the juice that can bring joy even when people are at their most tired and most stressed-out.

I t was after 11 p.m., the overbooked flight was already an hour late for takeoff, and the crowd was getting grumpy. If ever there was a chance to practice peace in the midst of annoyance, this was it.

Finally we were herded onto the plane and I settled into my seat, with hopes of getting some shuteye. As soon as we reached cruising altitude, the flight attendant's voice boomed over the P.A. system: "Ladies and gentlemen, one of our passengers would like to request your assistance with a special event he is planning when we land. Dave in seat 17B is going to propose to his girlfriend, who is meeting him at the gate. He would like you to help him deliver some flowers to her. If 24 of you would each get one rose from Dave and give it to his lady before he gets off the plane, you can participate in his proposal. Dave will show you a photo of Heidi . . . to make sure the right lady gets the flowers."

Ah, what a wonderful idea! I wanted to participate, but I was seated too far from Dave to get to a rose before the other passengers. When we landed, however, I was one of the first off the plane, and I positioned myself off to the side to watch the romantic spectacle.

Sure enough, there stood a lovely young woman waiting for her man. One by one, passengers exited the aircraft, each with a red rose in hand. With a smile, each person delivered a flower to Heidi, who shyly received them. Then the passengers formed a semi-circle behind Heidi, waiting for Dave and the Big Question.

Finally all the passengers had left the aircraft-except for Dave. The flight crew exited, but the groom-to-be was still conspicuously absent. Then the pilot and copilot emerged. They closed the door behind them, commenting, "Well, I guess that's it for the night." The crowd stood silently, watching, waiting, and hoping. Had Dave chickened out?

Suddenly, with all the aplomb of a Hollywood epic, the airplane door swung open one last time, now to reveal a handsome young man in a bright sailor suit. Dave had arrived. The audience breathed a welcome sigh of relief.

The knight in white, carrying yet another dozen red roses, strode proudly to his lady-in-waiting (who by now looked like Miss America, flowers piled to her nose). Tears streamed down her cheeks as she nervously watched her man approach, knowing full well what was about to happen.

Dave presented her with the flowers and ceremoniously dropped to one knee. The audience was rapt. By now it was nearly 1 a.m., but no one was going anywhere. Over 100 people fell silent and watched with awe.

Then he did it. He really did it. Dave produced a glittering gold ring and asked Heidi, "Will you marry me?" Of course she would. She tearfully nodded, and he slipped the ring onto her quivering fourth finger. With that, a great cheer and burst of applause went up from the jubilant crowd. The ovation reverberated through the silent airport, and probably still echoes today.

One by one, the group congratulated the couple, and then we all made our way toward baggage claim together. The corridor was filled with laughter, chatter, and storytelling. People were happy.

Then something very profound occurred to me: the entire crowd had been transformed. Over a hundred people who had been tired, impatient, and frazzled two hours earlier, were suddenly awake, joy-filled, and playing with each other. Such is the transformative power of one sincere expression of love.

We have been told that energy and fatigue depend on the time of day, how many hours of sleep we have had, stress, environment, age, and many other factors. Yet here was a group of people who had been awake for a long time, traveling under stressful conditions in an unnatural environment, yet they had more energy when they got off the plane than when they began!

Energy and happiness have little to do with what is going on around you, and a lot to do with what is going on inside you. You can find yourself in ideal conditions and be miserable, and you can be in the most adverse conditions and soar. Environment and physical factors may influence us, but attitude makes or breaks us. You may not be able to change your environment, but you can always change your mind.

Joy is the wild card of life; it supersedes every other formula for success. If you can find a way to create joy, you can rise beyond all external factors. If you can play at whatever you are doing, you are the master of your life. And if you should ever have the occasion to make a public proposal, you can take a planeload of 100 bugged and weary people, and turn their evening into a party they will never forget.

for reflection

In "A Public Proposal," Alan Cohen describes Spirit as manifesting itself in "one sincere expression of love"—it has the power to energize an entire planeload of tired, disgruntled travelers. Victor Frankl, in his book Man's Search for Meaning, talks about how one minute spent remembering a loving occasion in his life took away the pain of his brutal incarceration in a concentration camp.

Take a moment and close your eyes. Think about the last time you experienced the presence of love. Perhaps someone was with you? Perhaps you were alone. Perhaps you were in a garden and spent a moment thinking what a glorious day this is.

It's important to remember that the mind does not know the difference between what's real and imagined. We react emotionally and biologically to our thoughts as if we were actually experiencing what we're thinking about.

We've all had moments when we were touched by the presence of love. It doesn't matter what the situation was. For the time you felt love; you felt full, happy, and content. Close your eyes and reimagine that time. Where were you? Were you indoors or outdoors? Were you alone or was someone or more than one person with you? Can you smell anything? Can you hear anything? What are you wearing? Breathe deeply. Feel again what you were feeling that day.

As you relive this scene, watch as your breath becomes slower and more even. Become aware of a sense of relaxation spreading through your body as if you were letting down your guard. Be aware of joy rising up from your toes all the way to the crown of your head. Keep your focus on this image of joy for at least five minutes. Taking time to relax and focus on joy is healing. When the five minutes have passed, open your eyes slowly and notice how you feel. Like the passengers in Alan's story, you will feel refreshed and energized. That glorious feeling of being alive is Spirit moving through you.

Jump time

■ JEAN HOUSTON, PH.D.

Jean Houston is one of the founders of the human potential movement. For over thirty years, she has been writing, lecturing, and teaching about humanity's ability to achieve unlimited heights of creativity. Jean and her husband, Dr. Robert Masters, are the co-directors of the Foundation for Mind Research. The Foundation's goal is to explore the enhanced wisdom that studying the unconscious mind brings. Jean's list of accomplishments is endless. Buckminster Fuller once called her mind "a national treasure." She has written twenty books on physical and mental skills based on her research including *The Possible Human: A Course in Enhancing Your Physical, Mental, and Creative Abilities* and *Search for the Beloved*. Jean is the founder of the Mystery School, a program of cross-cultural mythic and spiritual studies. Additionally, Jean has introduced a new field called Social Artistry. As Program Director of the International Institute for Social Artistry, she works closely with the United Nations Development Program, offering programs in intensive training in social artistry for leaders in developing countries. Jean has worked personally with business, educational, and government leaders, including Senator Hillary Rodham Clinton, to help them clarify their goals.

In the following essay, Jean describes the times we're living in as Jump Time (which is also the title of one of her most recent books). Jump Time is a period of rapid evolutionary change. The rapid changes taking place in the world today may be disruptive, but Jean believes that they are acting as catalysts scraping away superficial veneers to reveal humanity's innate potential and fullest mental capacities.

Einstein said many years ago, "The consciousness that creates a problem cannot be the same kind of consciousness that solves it." Right now the biggest changes ever in human history are happening faster and faster. I call what is happening now Jump Time. Our minds, bodies, and souls have not been nurtured or prepared to deal with the complexity of problems that face us. So for me, nurturing involves the nurturing of all the latent talents and capacities that we have. We know that most people, given time, given training, given opportunity, become more creative and function beautifully. They've learned to heal themselves. They've learned to think. "The Possible Human" is no mere fantasy. I've worked with others for thirty-odd years and have shown that it it this within our grasp. I believe the kinds of challenges and complexities we have today are making us be more of what we can be.

We have an innate drive to get up in the morning and get going. It's the evolutionary drive. It's the wishing, yearning, longing, feeling this impulse from our souls to get on with it. And then of course there are the entrapments, the kinds of thoughts that say, "Oh, maybe next year when I feel better, when I lose weight, when I pay my taxes, I'll get on with my life." I think that most people, in my own experience, have that kind of double charge; that lure of becoming and that sense of galloping sloth. It's very good to nurture this evolutionary drive in what I call a teaching/learning community. The thing is that, if you have a community, the people in it will inspire and empower you and hold you to your task. One thing that I teach besides my regular work is how to build a developmental community; a community that really helps people nurture each other. I see this sense of commitment nurturing the globe.

I have a vision of people gathering together and volunteering to help each other. I see women slowly rising to full partnership with men. I see the way that new technology is permeating virtually every country so that we are being woven together in a great world mind that is taking on a life of its own.

Jump Time actually refers to a term used in evolutionary theory, *punctuated equilibrium*. Fossil records look pretty much the same for a very long time, sometimes millions of years. Then suddenly in relatively few generations—whoop—they jump into a whole new entity. The species suddenly acquires all kinds of new characteristics. This happens throughout evolution. Darwin hoped that we would find the missing link from one species to the new one, but we don't find it. So, many evolutionary theorists are assuming that there is what is called a "rapid phase transition." Well, I am suggesting that, given factors that are unique in human history, we are in such a Jump Time. Human beings may end up looking the way we do, but they may not be acting and feeling the same way. The new factors that are helping us are, of course, the change in the human consciousness, the change in human society, the breakdown and breakthrough of every way we used to know and think, and the breakdown of the membrane between peoples. Suddenly, as I had said, not only is history happening faster and faster, peoples and cultures are coming together. There's this vast conspiracy of sharing. Also there's a tremendous fascination with spirituality. So people are finding meditation and celebrating spirit in ways that they hadn't before. Of course perhaps this has something to do with a greater need that the earth has for this spirit at this time. Because, quite frankly, if we are the dominant species, we need to learn to nurture the earth. We cannot shrug our shoulders any longer.

You know, there are other aspects of our political side that you don't see on the media. Often the energy is moving elsewhere. It is moving from what I call politics to the original word that politics was derived from, *politeia,* which meant preserving the civil society; people getting together in groups, societies, and communities and really beginning to help and do for each other. The grassroots greening-of-community movement is a tremendous force, not just in this country, but in many societies of the world. It's almost as if people are beginning to take back their authentic powers and responsibilities. We need to look at where the creative order is going. I think it is going into a civil society. People are beginning to find organic ways of organizing the community for social benefit.

I think these are the most exciting times in human history. We've thought that other times were it, but we were wrong, this is it. I think it is very important that we nurture ourselves and each other to be stewards of this most exciting time.

for reflection

Jump Time is the speeding up of evolution that occurs from time to time during the course of history. Rather than a slow steady progression, changes within species or civilizations sometimes occur rapidly. Jean Houston suggests that the era we're living in is a Jump Time. This Jump Time is being precipitated by the breakdown of traditional forms of security like family and jobs. It is also precipitated by the increasing awareness that the health of human beings depends on the health of the earth. And, of course, the impulse of the Spirit within us pushes us to take responsibility and recreate our lives to meet the immediate challenges that Jump Time presents to us.

Have you been experiencing Jump Time?

Have you noticed that you're living your life at a faster pace?

Have you noticed that your life is changing faster than it ever has?

Are you becoming more aware that your thoughts, words and deeds have an impact on the world?

Has your focus changed over the past few years from a focus on self to a focus on self and community?

Are you listening to your soul's impulse as it calls you to nourish and heal our human community?

Enlightenment through entertainment

■ STEPHEN SIMON

Producer Stephen Simon is a beacon of spiritual light in the movie industry. His hit movies, including *Somewhere in Time* and *What Dreams May Come*, often have spiritual themes. Through the Spiritual Cinema Circle and his latest movie, *Indigo*, Simon is committed to making a difference in the world. He is also the author of *The Force Is with You: Mystical Movie Messages That Inspire Our Lives*. Simon's mission is to inspire people to be what human beings can be when we are at our best. To Simon, the word *spiritual* means "connecting to the unseen Divine essence that is the life force itself." As stated on his web site, www.spiritualcinema.com, "History has revealed that individuals or cultures that lose their connection to this essence become devoid of love, respect, and compassion."

Simon is also the co-founder and president of Moving Messages: The Institute for Spiritual Entertainment, Inc., an educational development and distribution non-profit corporation for feature films, television shows, documentaries, and educational and training programs. With a focus on spirituality and film, he teaches seminars and writes a nationally syndicated column called "The Movie Mystic."

Simon describes the nature of spiritual transformation that the world is going through and further discusses the contribution he is making to that transformation.

I was quoted recently as saying, "We're the ones we've been waiting for." What I meant by that is that humanity has to move on. As my friend Neale Donald Walsch says in his book, *Tomorrow's God,* there hasn't been a new idea in organized religion in over 2000 years. We have emerged from 2000 years of organized exclusionist religions into a time where we can move and are moving into an era of spirituality. In this era, we do not believe that anyone in the world has a right to an exclusive franchise on God.

The quote, "we're the ones we've been waiting for" isn't original, but comes from a wonderful message of the Hopi elders that went around the internet a couple of years ago. We are not waiting for the deliverance by a savior; that is for organized religions that are waiting for someone else to save them. We don't believe that we need saving. And whatever we need, we have within us when we connect with our own vision and our own version of God/Goddess/All That Is/Light/Spirit/the Universe— whatever you want to call it. We don't need Jesus to forgive us for our sins. We have the ability and the power to forgive ourselves. The time of the guru is over. The time has come for all of us to recognize that we have the ability to change our lives and to change the world within our own hearts, minds, souls, and instinctive knowledge through our connection to Spirit. And if you believe, as millions of people believe, that this experiment—this illusion—we call life is a conscious decision to return to a state of oneness, after having separated from it thousands and thousands of years ago, it gives new meaning to the fact that we are the ones we've been waiting for.

The age from which we are emerging has been dominated by religions that are oriented toward masculinity and struggle. These ideas are firmly entrenched and so it is very difficult to say, "I have a different destiny." Using the movie *Whale Rider* as a metaphor, what the main character does is to discover the real sense of her own destiny. She does this from a deeply feminine perspective, without confrontation and without ugliness. But in all ways, from the time she was born, she was totally committed to knowing her own destiny.

I believe that many of us feel that. I certainly did. I knew from the time I was very young that I would be doing exactly what I'm doing now. People thought I was crazy when I was in my teenage years, but I said to them that the best time of my life will be when I'm in my fifties. I believed that passionately because something within me knew that I was going to be doing exactly what I'm doing now. I feel so deeply honored and grateful to have spent my life getting ready to do what I'm doing now. All the failures, all the things that were so devastating and painful for me . . . I've been bankrupt. I've raised four daughters on my own for the last fifteen years. I've made more movies that lost money than have made money. I have been fired from three executive jobs in the film industry. I have known what it's like to have no money and no foreseeable future. There have been times in my life when literally every dollar I owned was in my pocket and that was not long ago. I learned from all of those situations and never ever gave up the vision of what I have now because it compelled me to move forward. I think there are many people on the planet today who have that same understanding: I came here to do something different, I came here to be something different; I came here to join a community with other people who are seeing life differently. I've known a lot of heartache and I've known a lot of failure in my life, but that does not make me a failure.

Choosing the things we do in life is the best example of creating our own reality. Each individual who is on a spiritual path, at some point or another, becomes conscious of the basic underlying bedrock of all metaphysics and all spiritual teachings that say that each individual creates his or her own reality—no exceptions. Every single thing that happens to us in our lives is a result of our choices. Sometimes those are elevated choices. Sometimes they are not. But we choose everything, not necessarily consciously all the time; we certainly wouldn't choose the heartbreak and failures many of us have known. But there is a part of us, and often it is the evolved part of us, that understands that there are certain experiences that we need to undergo in order to evolve in this lifetime on this planet. When you accept the fact that you create your own reality—and you create it every single day—it eliminates the possibility of looking at yourself as a victim. It is the most empowering, and at the same time, daunting recognition because you realize that you do have within you the power to create whatever reality you choose to create. That again means that the power is centered in the human heart and the human soul, not in some outside external power. That can be very hard when really very, very difficult things happen in life. But people that you and I know who are on a spiritual path, when something like that happens to them, they now ask, "Why did I create that in my life?" There is such a huge difference in that question versus: "Oh my God, why did you do this to me?" God doesn't do things to us. We do things to us and to each other. And instead of putting that power outside of us, if we understand that we're the ones we've been waiting for, then it's an extraordinarily powerful thing to know that we are literally able to change life on this planet.

My own particular small niche in all of this is to help create spiritual entertainment as a genre. And to help, along with thousands of other people, rehabilitate the word spiritually. When I started on this journey a few years ago, I wanted to call this genre spiritual cinema. Almost everybody I came into contact with told me to choose a different word other than spiritual. They said that people wouldn't understand it or they would think it's synonymous with religious, or a lot of people would have negative connotations, or that it means New Age.

But spiritual is the right word and people need to understand that its meaning is different from the word religious. You can be a very religious person and be spiritual, but you do not have to be religious to be spiritual. A part of my journey here is to bring this genre of Spiritual Entertainment out into a national and international dialog. To do this, our Institute is sponsoring programs, creating films, and distributing these films to bring more and more of this entertainment out into the world. The goal is to have people who are on a spiritual path have their own genre of entertainment that they can turn to. We don't want to replace anything or say that what we're doing is better than anything else, because it is not.

People go to the movies to be entertained. What we can do is entertain people and through that entertainment, bring in certain visions and ideas that people can connect with at their own pace and their own time, and ask their own questions about. For instance, my film *What Dreams May Come* is an epic after-life love story/adventure story about a man who wants to help his wife literally retrieve her own soul. It was meant to be a powerfully entertaining and moving movie. Underneath all that, it says things like thoughts are real; the physical world is the illusion, as well as other things. But those are things that people can discuss after the movie. Hopefully, they don't feel that the purpose of the film was to teach them something, because I think audiences resent that. What I believe, and what I counsel young filmmakers about all the time, is that your primary responsibility is to entertain people and to make them feel better about being human when they leave the theater than they did when they came in. And, underneath all that, if you can put in some interesting messages, that's great. You want people to enjoy the movie and than an hour later, while discussing the movie with a friend, relate some deeper insight that came to them as a result of watching the movie.

for reflection

One of Stephen Simon's ideas about spirituality is simply that we have separated ourselves from each other, and to return to the oneness that we all share is our path to our spiritual being and power.

Many icons fill Russian Orthodox churches. These icons are pictures of saints. The idea is to gaze upon the icon until you become one with the Saint, producing a feeling of great joy and peace. Those of the orthodox faith would call this a religious experience, but it can also be seen as a spiritual one because you're connecting with something larger than yourself.

Let's try this method of contemplation in a different context. Sit comfortably anywhere you like, inside or outside your home. Find an object, a vase, picture, lamp, tree, or the face of a loved one—it really does not matter what the symbol is . . . as long as you like it. This exercise should last no longer than five or ten minutes at the most.

Fill your eyes and mind with this object of value. Breathe deeply and relax as you gaze upon the object. Just relax. Relax, relax, relax. Blink whenever you feel it's necessary. Allow this object to flood your mind. You will soon feel filled with this object, and a feeling of oneness will flow in you, through you, and all around you. You will experience the great joy of the peace of God that passeth understanding.

Our children

■ NEALE DONALD WALSCH

Neale Donald Walsch has emerged as one of this country's most noted spiritual activists. His best-selling *Conversations with God* series (Books One, Two, and Three) and his books *Friendship with God* and *Communion with God* have been translated into thirty-four languages, extending his popularity around the globe.

Neale recently organized the Humanity Conference, which took place in Seoul, South Korea. The purpose of the program was "to seek planetary change to create a non-violent, more compassionate and sustainable world." His latest books are *The New Revelations, Tomorrow's God,* and *What God Wants.*

Neale is very candid about the fact that he is not a saint or a sage and does not want to be taken as a guru. He is committed to empowering other people to finding the truth within them. One way he is doing this is through his latest creation, Humanity's Team, a worldwide grassroots movement that Neale describes as "a Civil Rights Movement for the Soul, freeing humanity from the oppression of its beliefs about God, about Life, and about each other." Humanity's Team communities are being established throughout the world, allowing people to put spiritual principles into action in their own locales and in their relationships with their own families.

Neale's humanity is evidenced in his two contributions to *A Chorus of Wisdom.* In "Our Children," he urges us to remember our children's spiritual needs. At the same time, perhaps more importantly, he urges us to take time to nurture ourselves. Neale's second essay, "The Crisis of Compassion," follows immediately after "Our Children."

They may never say it, but children are spiritually hungry and depend on us to provide them with resources that bring spiritual development. For just as we hunger for a higher awareness and deeper understanding of the human adventure, so do children. But in order for us to nourish our children, our own lives must be nourished as well. We need to give ourselves time to relax, time to enjoy life, and time away from the extraordinary pressure and stress that modern technology has placed on our lives where we cannot get away from work. When we begin to nurture ourselves, we realize it is okay to give ourselves that extra bowl of ice cream even if it does mean we put on half a pound. When we nurture ourselves, we also give ourselves the chance to sit quietly and read a good book on a Sunday afternoon although there could be more practical things to do on the computer.

As nourished guardians or even guardian angels, we become better equipped to nourish our children and supply them with opportunities for their inner growth. We can place our children in front of the kinds of material that we would love to have them exposed to—the kinds of books, television programs, musical experiences of song and dance, and fine arts that will benefit them. We are also better equipped to see the importance of placing children in environments where they notice the lovely and joyous aspects of the human experience. Schools used to provide nourishment to children's souls through extraordinary programs in the art, music, and dance. But school budgets have been cut back, and such experiences are no longer as prevalent. As parents, as guardians, we must give ourselves time to be with our children, and to nurture our children by also nurturing ourselves.

It is up to us to lead our children into warm and wonderful and glorious places in their own life experiences. We have to deal candidly, openly, honestly, and compassionately with their fears, and always enhance their understanding of the possibility that their may be more going on here than any of us could possibly imagine. From the very early days of their lives, we have to help children to notice how to get in touch with the energy of the Divine, the universe, which we also call God. They need to be shown how to depend on God. And they need to know we can all experience communion with God, which is a sense of deep oneness and unity with the Divine. Children are spiritually hungry. Let us do everything to make sure their hunger is not ignored.

for reflection

Nurturing has no boundaries. We nurture our children and everyone in our lives by nurturing ourselves.

We nurture each other by sharing food and love. But children also need spiritual nourishment. If you have children, ask yourself how you can enrich their lives through the arts and entertainment. How can you inspire them to connect to Spirit to allow them to express themselves creatively?

Are you also allowing your children to talk about their fears without diminishing or exaggerating them? Do you share your *fears with your children, as well as the process you use to over-come your fears?*

Are you taking time to nourish yourself by taking time for rest and relaxation and allowing yourself an occasional extra bowl of ice cream? Living from Spirit means that we treat ourselves gently like the children of God that we are.

The crisis of compassion

■ NEALE DONALD WALSCH

In Neale's second essay, "The Crisis of Compassion," he asks us to recognize that the world is truly a global village; it is an interconnected whole, where one part affects every other part.

I think it should first be made clear that coming from love does not mean that one does not do anything. Especially among the mainstream media, every time a New Thought or a New Age person says "we should come from love," the immediate assumption is that we mean people should do nothing but sit back at home and light a candle and pray. It is not loving to the abuser nor to the abused for one to allow the abuse to continue. So it is loving to teach a person who is acting inappropriately that his actions are considered inappropriate and he needs to stop them now. It certainly is loving for us to do that with children. Why wouldn't it be loving for us to that with adults?

What method can we use to love a person into more appropriate behavior? The answer is, whatever method works. *Conversations with God* says that a highly evolved society should ask itself what its goals are, and what works and what doesn't work in achieving those goals. For a Global Village that is trying to live life in peace and harmony, it doesn't work to permit people to fly airplanes into buildings. What we need to say to those people who fly airplanes into buildings is "I'm sorry, but you can't do that."

However, as a Global Village, we have to ask ourselves what it is about U.S. policies that doesn't work, if we want to live a life of peace and harmony. We would then identify those behaviors that we engage in that could cause others to want to attack us or want to support those who attack us. This in no way condones any terrorist attacks. What it does suggest is that if we looked at that question as fairly and as objectively as we looked at the first question (what in their behaviors does not work), we might just come up with a mutually-agreed-upon solution. One thing that clearly does not work is for 2 percent of the world's population to hold 95 percent of the world's resources and wealth. We have reached a point on this planet where the other 98 percent of the world's people are no longer willing to sit by and allow that disparity to exist without making some kind of statement about it.

One has to understand, too, the Muslim experience in many countries of the world. They have too often been marginalized and not given a voice in the creation of their own experience. Many Muslims live in oil-rich Arab countries controlled and dominated by governments that give the average Muslim on the street little voice, if any, in their own daily affairs. The resulting societies are repressive: all dissenting voices are quieted and all outspokenness is discouraged and in fact disallowed. In many of those countries, the only outlet for an aggrieved person is to express their grief through religion, run, unless our cultural story itself—the beliefs from which behavior emerges—is altered.

We have to change our thinking about how life is lived. We have to change the pattern of our behavior, and behavior patterns are only changed when thinking patterns are changed. We have to think in a new way about governments, economics, and life itself. We have to think new thoughts about God and ourselves and our relationships with all other people on the planet. Simply put, we have to have a new idea about who all of us are in relationship to each other on the earth. The ideas we currently hold in our head are no longer relevant.

September 11th is the outfall not of a political crisis, nor of an economic crisis; it is the outfall of a spiritual crisis. The problem is that people all over the world understand what compassion is, but we have abandoned our willingness to express it. That's the crisis. We face a crisis of compassion on the planet.

because that is the one right that even the most de
ernments and monarchies will not violate. Most go
understand that if you violate the right to religious e>
it could cause a revolution that would be turned ag
government itself.

What has happened in many Muslim countries
governments have collaborated with religion and have b
the sponsors of religions. If you look to see who are the Ir
in many parts of the Arab world (an Imam is the relig
leader of a given mosque), you find that they are appointec
the government. So, people feel they cannot even trust th
mainstream religious leaders, causing them to turn to other u
orthodox and far more radical religious groups who have turne
Islam into a political as well as a religious and spiritual movement

The first thing we need to do to solve these problems is to
create a viable outlet for spiritual and political resolution of the
social problems faced by people in those countries. That will
never happen so long as despotic or beneficial monarchies rule
over the people. Many Arabs are furious with the United States
for seeming to support such governments.

What can one do? The real issue is a shift of consciousness.
Consciousness creates behavior and behavior creates social policy.
The solution lies at the level of belief. We keep trying to create
the solution at the level of behavior; if you would just do things
differently, then the outcome would be other than what it currently is. We keep trying to create an environment in which
human beings do things differently, and human beings will
never do things differently in the long run, only in the short

for reflection

Neale Donald Walsch tells us that we face a new crisis on this planet, a crisis of compassion. What's missing from our lives is the expression of concern and caring for our fellow inhabitants of this planet. Compassion is a state of mind, and in order to become a compassionate person we must shift our consciousness from getting to sharing. This new consciousness, acted upon lovingly, can save this world from self destruction.

The path to a compassionate mind is not one of meditation, but rather one of action. A creative act of compassion, love, or caring for someone or something other than ourselves brings us to the spiritual part of mind, the God part of mind, the part of mind that connects each and every one of us. Every act of compassion is a strand in the web of communion that binds us together in unconditional love.

The steps in creating a compassionate state of mind are very simple. Start with the most obvious. Look around at your environment. Notice the people there, and remember, an act of compassion is an act of love or caring. You might anonymously leave a rose on a fellow workers desk, allow a car entering the highway to get in front of you as a courtesy, greet someone who seems to be down with a smile, or send a check to the Red Cross for disaster relief in a far off country.

If you can discipline yourself to create one act of compassion everyday, you'll find that you have made a habit of mind that will raise you to a level of peace, love, understanding, and connectedness that will be sensed and loved by the people that surround you.

living with *mortality*

Finding inner peace

■ GERALD G. JAMPOLSKY, M.D.

Jerry Jampolsky is the author of over a dozen books that deal with self-healing. Jerry has the ability to communicate spiritual concepts clearly and simply, but without losing their depth. Jerry's landmark book, *Love Is Letting Go of Fear*, helped spur the growing interest in spirituality that has been going on for the past thirty years. Jerry is the founder of the Center for Attitudinal Healing. The Center is a place where children and adults facing life-threatening illness go to find peace of mind. There are now more than 130 independent Centers for Attitudinal Healing found in twenty-four countries. The twelve principles of attitudinal healing can be found in Jerry's recently re-released book, *Teach Only Love*. Jerry and his wife, Diane Cirincione, Ph.D., lecture internationally on the profound effects of attitudes on the quality of people's lives.

Jerry teaches that when all we want is the peace of God, then the barriers between our spiritual lives, personal lives, and work lives dissolve. Jerry's work reflects the humility of one who is walking the path of awareness and has made mistakes, learned from them, and gone on.

One day in meditation I received some very strong guidance to start a small group for children who were facing death and apply the principles of *A Course in Miracles* to this group. The group turned out to be wise spiritual elders in young, small bodies, who came to teach me, and the volunteers, another way of looking at life and another way of looking at death. At the time I was afraid of dying, but at the same time I was killing myself with alcohol.

Of course, my guide *A Course in Miracles* is all about how we are not bodies, we are spiritual beings. Since 1975 I have been repeating the following prayer from the Course every morning when I wake up:

> I am not a body I am free for I am still as God created me.
> I want the Peace of God
> The Peace of God is everything I want.
> The aim of all my living here, the end I seek, my purpose,
> my function, my life,
> while I abide where I am not at home.

That is the rudder that points my ship in the direction of peace: the peace of God is my only goal. More and more, over time, I see people as light beings. I had a dream four years after starting the Center for Attitudinal Healing. I was on a hilltop. At that time, I had been with almost every one of our children at the time of their death. In the dream I was with every child who had died, and we were dancing in a circle. They started moving away from the ground, while I stayed on the ground, and they turned into light. It was a very beautiful dream. When I woke up, the dream seemed to be telling me that I'm on the right path—that this is not real, these bodies aren't real, and we truly are light beings. The reason we're here is to enlighten each other and extend the light of love to everyone.

We live in a world where most of the people witness to each other "we're bodies." And we think that when the body dies, that's the end of communication. The ego believes you're born only to die and that's the end of life. Whereas on a spiritual path we would say light, love, and life are the same thing, and that life is eternal. When we let go of our attachments, and see no separation between God and ourselves, there's just oneness. And that oneness has nothing to do with the material world. We get light and peace when we let go of the ego system and learn the value of letting go or forgiving others—turning to the light instead of blaming others, and letting go of the illusion that we're separate.

What we don't realize is that the truth is in our minds: the only problem in the world is that we've forgotten who we are. And, of course, we're not guilty because we've forgotten. The question I would ask anyone is, "How much do you want to experience the peace of God?" When you totally want the peace of God, then there is no difference between your work life, your personal life, and your sleep life. Dissolve the barriers between them with your intentions. We all make mistakes. It's just an error to be corrected.

I've been around a lot of holy people: I've been around Mother Theresa thirteen or fourteen times and I've seen her angry. I've seen the Dali Lama get upset. I've seen the same with Baba Muktananda. So, I don't know anyone who doesn't make mistakes. A very helpful question to ask is, "What can I do in this second, to reexperience the peace of God?"

Our attachment to anger makes us feel that anger will bring us something that we want or desire. The attachment to our ego is the attachment to fear, murder, and war. When we see only the value in loving, when we see only the value in having two emotions, seeing another person as either loving or fearful—and seeing fear as a call for help—then our hearts automatically open. I'm in the middle of doing a new book right now called *Shortcuts to God*. There are lots of cartoons in it by a friend of mine, Leslie Vargas. One of the cartoons has a sort of a picture of me and there's a door that says GOD on it. The cartoon figure is trying to open the door, and he's sweating, and sweating, and sweating, and he just can't get the door open. What he doesn't realize is that he's putting his foot against the door. A lot of us put our foot against the door by making judgments, observing people's behavior, thinking we're better than other people. As soon as we take our foot off the door, we see that God is with us all the time. My goal is not to try to change people, but to try to have the peace of God as my only goal.

I'm not trying to fix people up. When you're trying to fix people up, then it's very difficult. My goal is not the outcome. My goal is that whatever I'm doing with that person right now, I'm doing with love.

If you still want to save them, then you're going to come into conflict again. You're trying to change them. *A Course in Miracles* is trying to say, "Hey, anything you see is just a part of an illusion, and we're not trying to change the illusion; we're trying to let go of the illusion."

It's easy to see suffering, but we can go past that. If you continue to see the light in that person, then you will not see the suffering. Your physical eyes are seeing the costume that's suffering. If for a moment you look with Christ eyes, then you're not going to see suffering, you're going to see a light and love in them.

for reflection

Jerry Jampolsky believes in experiencing the peace of God right here and now. In order to do that, we have to let go of future expectations, past grievances and present fears. These feelings become the veils of ignorance that cloud our eyes and keep us from seeing the light in our souls and each other.

Make yourself comfortable. Unwind. Relax your fingers your toes, relax your legs, your abdomen, your chest, your arms, your neck and your head. Allow any grievance that you hold, any lack of forgiveness you still resent to enter your mind. Say to yourself, "I want my soul to be free of these imprisoning thoughts." Allow yourself to see these negative thoughts fall deeper and deeper and deeper yet, until they all are lost in the dark abyss. Take a deep breath. Ask your spirit to help you remember who you really are, a being of light whose home is in God. Open your eyes in peace and joy.

Lessons learned from accepting our mortality

■ BERNIE SIEGEL, M.D.

Dr. Bernie Siegel is a pioneer in the field of mind/body medicine. It may be more appropriate to call his work heart/body medicine, because he prescribes love as an adjunct in the healing process. His first book, *Love, Medicine and Miracles,* helped bring holistic ideas on health and healing to the mainstream. Bernie's more recent books include *Help Me to Heal* and *365 Prescriptions for the Soul* as well as a children's book, *Smudge Bunny.* His latest project is *101 Exercises for the Soul.*

In 1978 he originated Exceptional Cancer Patients, a specific form of individual and group therapy utilizing patients' drawings, dreams, images and feelings. ECaP is based on "carefrontation," a safe, loving therapeutic confrontation, which facilitates personal lifestyle changes, personal empowerment and healing of the individual's life. The ECaP patients experienced tremendous physical, spiritual and psychological benefits. These results led Bernie to want to make everyone aware of his or her own healing potential.

That year, he began talking about patient empowerment and the choice to live fully and die in peace. As a physician, who has cared for and counseled innumerable people who's mortality has been threatened by an illness, Bernie embraces a philosophy of living and dying that stands at the forefront of the medical ethics and spiritual issues our society grapples with today. He continues to assist in the breaking of new ground in the field of healing and personally struggling to live the message of kindness and love.

Acceptance of your mortality can bring you subtle inner peace. When you realize what is truly important, there aren't too many things that can make you lose your peace of mind, and your authentic journey begins at that point. This is what I have found in my life and the lives of the people I care for. On a therapeutic level, when people say, "Yes, I'm mortal," and begin to do what they want to do with their remaining lifetime, it's amazing the physical benefits they derive from living their chocolate ice cream. Once they say, "Yes, I'm mortal," and change their lives, the physical benefits are the side effect I read about expressed in letters saying, "I forgot to die because I felt so good leading this new life."

Once you accept and begin to live your true life you derive physical, as well as spiritual and psychological benefits. There are many paths to health and wholeness, but there's only one path for each individual. In other words, I can be a doctor, somebody can be a plumber, housewife, carpenter, or landscaper. They're saying, "This is my way of contributing love to the world. This is my path to health and wholeness because this is how I help people." But what you will find is that the path comes from your inner happiness, and that's how you find your path, not from the intellect. That is how to save your life and not lose it, as all the spiritual leaders tell us.

There are many ways to express this: the Way, the Tao, the Halakah, the path; Christ talks about narrow gates and wide gates. The meaning of the word *evil* was originally derived from "to lose your way." So no matter what philosophies you study, they all tell us how to find our way. And your body is a wonderful guide too. If it doesn't feel good, you're off your path and losing your way. Your life isn't about what you think is good for you, or what you think you ought to do today, or what you think you ought to become; it's what feels right for you to do with your lifetime. When you do, then you will find your path and will live your longest, healthiest life and feel successful.

What we are learning from the patients I work with is survival behavior. The word *patient* means "a sufferer," so if you're a submissive sufferer, you will do poorly in the hospital, but everybody will be glad that you're there because you don't cause any trouble . . . if you speak up and ask questions, you are more likely to survive, but the staff may have a poor opinion of you. What I'm teaching people is what I call survival behavior. Whether it's AIDS, cancer, being fired, divorced, in a concentration camp, or on a sinking ship, there are behaviors and attitudes that can help you survive. Most of the books about surviving are by people who've been through their own personal hell and learned the hard way, by becoming strong at their broken places.

"To live is to suffer. To survive is to find meaning in the suffering." These statements are by Victor Frankl, a prisoner in a Nazi concentration camp, who saved his life by giving love. Frankl decided that he was going to survive and write a book about this experience and make it meaningful because he didn't want this to happen again.

There is essential and nonessential suffering. Most of the suffering we go through is totally unnecessary. We bring it upon ourselves, and this is something I try to teach our family. Do not let other people control your thoughts. If you're waking up every morning upset, angry, or miserable because of what someone else has done, they are still in charge of your life. Abandon your past and don't let it control your life and feelings, because you don't have life time to waste being miserable. Let your pain protect you and lead you to seek to nourish yourself and your life, as you seek food when hungry. Then you will not suffer and experience meaningless pain. When you feel loved, everything hurts less.

When you have a schedule and reservations, you get caught up in the nonsense and lose track of the universe's schedule. You have to let go and let God and live in the moment. If you miss a plane, give it up; surrender and live where you are right now. Everything is fine. Especially if the plane you miss crashes. That's just being the loving *human being* that God created, and not a *human doing*. When you can bring love into any situation, you will be amazed at what you're capable of doing and how beautifully things turn out. When we choose love, we create one family, so that we are not killing each other over colors, races, religions, sexes. We are all one family. All the same color inside and blind to faults because of our love.

for reflection

Dr. Bernie Siegel notes that accepting your own mortality brings you inner peace. Many people shy away from thinking about death because it scares them. What they don't realize is simply that this kind of acceptance brings one physical, psychological and spiritual benefits. In other words, it makes you a healthier person right now.

Sit in a comfortable position in a chair, close your eyes, and relax your body part by part, starting with your feet. Say out loud, "Feet relax, relax, relax, relax, feet relax." Continue on to your ankles, knees, thighs, belly, back, arms, shoulders, neck and head. Your body is totally relaxed.

See in your mind the faces of some people you admire who have passed on, who have left their bodies and gone to another dimension. The reason we admire people like Mahatma Gandhi, Mother Teresa, Albert Einstein, Martin Luther King, Jr., Thomas E. Jefferson, etc. is that they all had purpose in their lives. This purpose animated them and was far stronger than any fear they experienced, including the fear of death. You, too, have a purpose that is larger than the fear of death and larger than you personally, which is your gift to the planet. Focus for a moment on your purpose; see it written large in fiery letters in your mind. Read each word aloud. This purpose, be it compassion, adventure, creation or service will follow you when your body leaves this plane. Your purpose is immortal and so is your spirit. We really don't die, we move on to a different level of spiritual existence.

We are all God

■ JAMES VAN PRAAGH

James Van Praagh is one of the most gifted mediums of our time. He is both clairsentient and clairvoyant; he can hear and see people in the spirit world. More than that, he's able to feel their emotions. But his real gift is the ability to communicate the messages he hears, sees, and feels, to the spirits loved ones who are in this world.

James is a very popular TV talk show figure; he has appeared on *Oprah*, *Larry King Live*, *Maury Povich*, *20/20*, *48 Hours*, and *The Other Side*. In his best-selling book *Talking to Heaven*, James defines being psychic as being connected to one's soul. He believes that we all have the potential to be psychic by developing our own "inner knowingness" and attuning to our feelings. To do that, though, means learning to listen to our own instincts and intuitions and breaking out of our learned conditioning. He offers "how to" processes in his latest book *Meditations with James Van Praagh*.

James' essay is a concise, gentle exploration of life and death: Why are we here? What happens when we die? James reminds us that we are spirit. When we turn to our spiritual reality for answers, we become less sidetracked as we follow our path.

People are increasingly becoming interested in psychic phenomena, mediumship, and spirituality. They're looking for answers. They want to know what their lives are about, why they are here, and what lies in their future. They also want to alleviate their fear of death. Through the exploration of psychic phenomena, they will find that there is no such thing as death.

Things don't change overnight. It's a process. It's now becoming okay to believe these kinds of things. A few years ago, NBC ran a show called *The Others*. Now NBC is running *The Medium*. I also believe that the children being born now are much more open to these ideas. The rules are not as rigid now as when we were growing up. People realize that religion doesn't answer all the questions anymore.

People are learning that everything is energy. Thoughts, words, and deeds are energy. Just because you don't see a thought, it doesn't mean that it doesn't exist. We have radio stations and we receive the signals on our radios. But the signals are unseen with the physical eye, even though they exist. They must exist, because we have voices and music coming out of the radio. Telephone and television transmission are also based on waves of energy. You cannot see these energy waves, but they exist. Thought operates in the same way. Every thought has an energy frequency attached to it. Like attracts like. If you have negative thoughts within yourself, you will create negative things. There's a wonderful book called *As a Man Thinketh* by James Allen. It's about what how we create what we think.

We all are God, and God is constantly creating, so we're always filled with creative energy. God always says "Yes," but we, our egos, say "No." Our egos are limiting. The physical world is limiting. It's a dense world. But when you turn to your God self, you see the higher level of who you really are. So if you fill yourself with self-destructive thinking like, "I can't do this, I'm not good enough, I'm not smart enough, I'm not good looking enough, I'm ugly, and I'll never get that job," your experience will reflect that.

The physical body is only an encasement; you are spirit and you'll always be spirit. You are also energy, and energy cannot die. You cannot kill energy. Your spirit is made up of all of who you are, everything you've thought about, who you are, your ambitions, etc. When you die, you take that with you. The only thing you leave behind is your physicality. In the spirit world, you're in a state of conscious awareness because you're closer to your true source. But, as I said, you've also brought with you those conditions that you had on the earth. If you felt badly about yourself, you'll experience that; if you were an alcoholic, you'll pass over with the sense of "I have to get a drink." Or a drug addict will think, "I have to get drugs." When you pass over those thoughts will be strong because you think they are a part of you. But they really are not; they are only a part of your earth mind.

There are counselors in the spirit world who have the job of counseling people who cross over to help them change their mindset. These counselors work with people who have crossed over with thoughts of suicide, unforgiveness, and guilt to help free them. A lot of people pass over who are in shock. They're in shock because they have hurt someone. They're in shock because they haven't loved themselves enough or loved someone else enough. Many people are stuck in that. They have to be willing, on their own, to move on and forgive themselves. Each person moves on in his or her own time. They can't be forced. The same thing happens on earth. We can give people as many spiritual books as we want; we can give them as much evidence about life after death—I can give them names and places and details and they could be incredibly accurate—but that person has to take the information and decide for himself if it makes sense. If something resonates as truth within them, then they can make the decision to make choices that will change things in their lives.

It's very difficult to watch people die, because we love them. In reality, they're much better off leaving the physical plan than being stuck here, because the nonphysical realm is our home. The physical realm is not our home. There's a lovely story told by a hospice nurse about a six-year-old boy who had cancer. He used to dream about a very peaceful garden with a crystal castle. He loved going there. He said that all his friends, who were in chemo with him, were also there and that they all played with each other. He said he wanted to go there. He stopped his treatment and very calmly died in his mother's arms.

I believe that before you come back into this incarnation, you set up a scenario. It's like there's a road in the forest and you've chosen to walk from one end to the other, wherever that is. Along the way, there will be paths that lead off to the side, and you can decide to go down a path and check it. What you will find is that the sidetrack won't meet your needs, and you'll have to go back to the original path. If you have a flashlight, maybe you'll find that original path easier. What I'm saying is that the more you know yourself, the easier it is to follow your path. You will have both good and bad experiences, but your job is to learn from both of them. That's how we develop. The more you become aware of who you are, which is spirit, and the more you listen to that inner knowledge, or that God self, the quicker you'll learn what you need to learn. You will make different choices. Your choices will be based on love.

The truth is very simple. People want complexities, but the truth is very simple. Love is all there is. There are only two ways of living life, and every single thing in life is derived from these two things: fear or love. That's all it comes down to, fear and love. Every single decision in life is made from those two things. I'm talking about decisions like whether to go to war, or balancing a budget. Whatever the decision is, it comes out of fear or love.

for reflection

James Van Praagh believes we are all part of God and that the God part of us is immortal. He also believes that we come into this incarnation with a path to follow. We become frustrated and mentally imprisoned if we are seduced into following other people's paths.

The way to the "God" part of us is our own intuition. If we use our intuition to make decisions, then those decisions will be made from love. If we allow our ego selves to make a decision then that decision will be coming from fear.

Sit quietly and close your eyes. Visualize in your mind the important crossroads of your life. Look at the choices you made at those crossroads or turning points. Which decisions were made from love? Which decisions were made from fear? Now see yourself in the present time. Choices are coming up every day. Look at the choices available to you right now. Cancel any decision coming from fear, hold on tightly to any decision that comes from love, because that is what you are.

conclusion

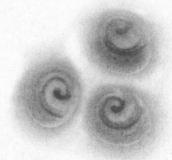

Conclusion

■ SORAH DUBITSKY, PH.D.

Years ago I took a "How to Write Your Memoirs" course. The instructor taught that our lives are like a novel. Every novel has a hero or heroine who wants something. The novel's plot consists of all the obstacles the heroine has to overcome in order to get what she wants. Spiritual living is like that. We are each the hero or heroine of our own life's story. Take a moment to think about your own life. What's the major theme of your life's story? Is it an adventure story like an Indiana Jones movie, or is it a romance novel? Is your central theme about making money or finding success? In most satisfying novels I've read, at the end of the story, regardless of whether the heroine has gotten what she wants, she has learned something. She has grown in the process. She has reached deep within herself and drawn up resources that she never knew she had. She had to confront her fears, doubts, and worries. In the process she discovered her wholeness. The authors in *A Chorus of Wisdom* have shared their insights about how spiritual living lifts them above the fray. It gives their lives meaning and purpose. It gives them the courage to live their visions. They realize that they are the creators of their life's experiences. But most importantly, they realize that their mission here is to love. In sharing that love, they have touched millions and millions of people.

I hope *A Chorus of Wisdom* has inspired you to see your life as the laboratory of your own spiritual awakening. To borrow a phrase, spiritual living is living from the inside out. It's not easy. It takes trust, faith, and courage. It means continuously turning within for answers. Sometimes those answers appear in the form of guides who show up at the most appropriate moments to point us in the right direction. That has been what each of the people in this book has been to me. Each one has shown up to answer some question I was asking, at the moment I was asking it, that helped guide me on my journey.

We are so fortunate to live in an age with such easy accesses to spiritual enlightenment. I know I need all the help I can get. A perfect example of getting help when I needed it is the poem below written by Stephen Levine. It came to me at one of those moments when I needed a shot of inspiration just to keep going. I hope it inspires you.

Trust your vision
Make it whole
    Hold it like the Navaho
    His solemn desert oracle
    In quest of shaman passage
    Gaining his healing chant
    Guiding him through life

Hold the vision
> Constantly rising
> It is the way nature works
> Through you
> It is the only self
> An ever-changing underdream
>> A vision (if you see it)
>> Up to you
>> To make it real.

Act on your vision
> And pray that you are blessed

Namaste

Appendix

All of the authors who contributed to *A Chorus of Wisdom* have web sites you can visit. Here are the addresses.

Marc Allen   www.MarcAllen.com, www.successwithease.com

Wally "Famous" Amos   www.chipandcookie.com

Steve Bhaerman   www.wakeuplaughing.com

Ma Jaya Sati Bhagavati   www.kashi.org

Jack Canfield   www.jackcanfield.com

Diane Cirincione, Ph.D.   www.healingcenter.org

Alan Cohen   www.alancohen.com

Barbara De Angelis, Ph.D.   www.barbaradeangelis.com

Armand DiMele   www.thepositivemind.com

Larry Dossey, M.D.   www.dosseydossey.com

Larry Dubitsky   www.larrydubitsky.com

Sorah Dubitsky, Ph.D. (editor)   www.drsorah.com

Gloria Estefan	www.gloriaestefan.com
Debbie Ford	www.debbieford.com
Rev. Edwene Gaines	www.prosperityproducts.com
Arlo Guthrie	www.arlo.net & www.guthriecenter.org
Gerald G. Jampolsky, M.D.	www.healingcenter.org
Jean Houston, Ph.D.	www.jeanhouston.org
Nathan Katz, Ph.D.	www.indojudaic.com
Hans Christian King	www.hansking.com
Stephen and Ondrea Levine	www.warmrocktapes.com
Judith Light	www.judithlight.com
Caroline Myss, Ph.D.	www.myss.com
John Perkins	www.johnperkins.org
Rabbi Chaim Richter	RichterCD@aol.com
Bernie Siegel, M.D.	www.ecap-online.org
Stephen Simon	www.spiritualcinemacircle.com
Toby Thompkins	www.tobyspeaks.com
James Van Praagh	www.vanpraagh.com
Dan Wakefield	www.danwakefield.com
Neale Donald Walsch	www.cwg.org

continuation of copyright page:

Foreword copyright © 2005 by Stephen and Ondrea Levine

"What It Means to Be Spiritual" copyright © 2005 by Gloria Estefan

"Do Something" copyright © 2005 by Arlo Guthrie

"Following the Spiritual Impulse" copyright © 2005 by Nathan Katz, Ph.D.

"Walking the Talk" copyright © 2005 by Judith Light

"Being a Spiritual Man" copyright © 2005 by Toby Thompkins

"Nurturing the Spiritual Spark" copyright © 2005 by Dan Wakefield

"Consciousness and Money" copyright © 2005 by Marc Allen

"Making Our Dreams Come True" copyright © 2005 by Jack Canfield

"Creativity and Prosperity" copyright © 2005 by Rev. Edwene Gaines

"Realizing One's Dreams" copyright © 2005 by John Perkins

"Creating Sacred Relationships" copyright © 2005 by Diane Cirincione, Ph.D. and Gerald G. Jampolsky, M.D.

"Spirituality, Intimacy, and Creating Real Relationships" copyright © 2005 by Armand DiMele

"You Are Enough As You Are" copyright © 2005 by Hans Christian King

"Relationships As a Spiritual Practice" copyright © 2005 by Stephen and Ondrea Levine

"Be the Message" copyright © 2005 by Wally "Famous" Amos

"Enlighten Up: Laughter As a Spiritual Path" copyright © 2005 by Steve Bhaerman

"Ten Ways to Wake Up Laughing—and Leave Laughter in Your Wake" copyright © 2005 by Steve Bhaerman

"Living a Conscious Life" copyright © 2005 by Barbara De Angelis, Ph.D.

"Revealing Your True Beauty" copyright © 2005 by Larry Dubitsky

"Authenticity" copyright © 2005 by Debbie Ford

"Healing" copyright © 2005 by Caroline Myss, Ph.D.

"Reinventing Medicine" copyright © 2005 by Larry Dossey, M.D.

"Aging with Purpose" copyright © 2005 by Rabbi Chaim Richter

"The World Needs Mothering" copyright © 2005 by Ma Jaya Sati Bhagavati

"A Public Proposal" copyright © 2005 by Alan Cohen

"Jump Time" copyright © 2005 by Jean Houston, Ph.D.

"Enlightenment Through Entertainment" copyright © 2005 by Stephen Simon

"Our Children" copyright © 2005 by Donald Walsch

"The Crisis of Compassion" copyright © 2005 by Neale Donald Walsch

"Finding Inner Peace" copyright © 2005 by Gerald G. Jampolsky, M.D.

"Lessons Learned from Accepting Our Mortality" copyright © 2005 by Bernie Siegel, M.D.

"We Are All God" copyright © 2005 by James Van Praagh

Acknowledgments

I want to acknowledge all the contributors to this volume. Thank you all for working with me and trusting me with your words. I'll use them for the highest and best purposes in service of humanity.

Thank you, too, to my husband, Larry Dubitsky, for his unending faith in me.

Special thanks to Andrea Hurst, my agent, who believed in this book. And thank you Dr. Bernie Siegel for referring me to Andrea. You have no idea what your writing in *Miracle Journeys* has meant to me over the years.

To Stephen and Ondrea Levine, I am inspired by your depth of your heart and the generosity of your spirit.

To my friends and family on the path, Marlena Lechner, Heidi Rosaler, Connie and Jerry Stern, Glenda Schwartz, Monika Sambell, Sherrie Miller, Christine Burkhardt, and Karyn Altman, thank you for being my healers, teachers, and confessors. To my publicist, Celina Klee, thank you for being sooooooo positive.

To Ashley Chase, at Ulysses Press, thank you for your patience.

And thanks to my Web Goddess, Mary Lou Pessoa.